DIVIDED
WE STAND

Library of Congress Cataloging-in-Publication Data

Ben-Porat, Amir.
  Divided we stand : class structure in Israel from 1948 to the
1980s / Amir Ben-Porat.
    p.   cm. — (Contributions in sociology, ISSN 0084-9278 ; no.
85)
  Bibliography: p.
  Includes index.
  ISBN 0-313-26402-3 (lib. bdg. : alk. paper)
  1. Social classes—Israel. 2. Social classes—Israel—Statistics.
3. Israel—Social conditions. I. Title. II. Series.
HN660.Z9S63   1989
305.5'095694—dc20   89-7493

British Library Cataloguing in Publication Data is available.

Library of Congress Catalog Card Number: 89-7493
ISBN: 0-313-26402-3
ISSN: 0084-9278

First published in 1989

Greenwood Press, Inc.
88 Post Road West, Westport, Connecticut 06881

Printed in the United States of America

The paper used in this book complies with the
Permanent Paper Standard issued by the National
Information Standards Organization (Z39.48-1984).

10 9 8 7 6 5 4 3 2 1

Contents

Acknowledgments

This book was written while I was on sabbatical at James Madison University in Harrisonburg, Virginia, where I had the good fortune to be helped by a great many people. In an atmosphere of both teaching and study I was able to devote my time to writing and listening. Let me take this opportunity to express my gratitude to the members of the department of sociology-anthropology and social work. I could not have found better colleagues for support and friendship.

The language editing of this book was carried out by A. Schotz, of Ben-Gurion University of the Negev, Israel. His professionalism and devotion were indispensible. Camera-ready copy was prepared by "WordByte" of Beer-Sheva.

List of Tables

Preface

Four decades of Israeli statehood have been troubled by nationalistic, cultural and ethnic conflicts that still abound. The least conspicuous of all these has been the class struggle, although, judging by the ratio of strikes, lockouts, other indicators of labor relations, and related political repercussions, some class struggle has been evident. However, when this became an issue on the political agenda, it was actually a limited and temporary conflict of workers and private, or public-state, employers. It never developed into a cleavage between classes "for themselves."

This lack of class struggle may be considered natural by some but astonishing by others. The answer lies in the political instance, or more precisely, the position of the political vis-a-vis other instances of the society. The Jewish political regime immediately after statehood remained as before, formed by agents from the social-democratic stream who were also Zionist-nationalistic. This regime was able to tame class conflict and, on more than a few occasions, to mobilize class power and class organizations toward nationalistic aims. The state, as this book shows, constituted the predominant social agent throughout the period studied and was therefore in a position to supervise class struggle within the boundaries of certain rules of the game. This was possible either by direct control or through cooperation with the trade unions.

But even the state could not hold back the process of class structure formation "in itself." The processes of state building, industrialization and growth were all related effects of a more primary process, that of transition toward a capitalist system. It was obviously affected by the specific conditions of the Israeli conjuncture, but in basic aspects, was similar to capitalist development in other places. The bottom line is that the process of transition toward a capitalist system is interwoven with that of class structure formation. As with the process of transition, that of class formation is also affected by the specificities of the particular (sociohistorical) conditions. Thus, it is a research study's task to reach a conclusion on the particular form and content of the class structure in a specific society. This is the main issue of this study.

The book is based on two different sources. One source is information on the economy and other areas of Israeli society from 1948 to the middle of the 1980s. The second source is information on the positions of individuals in the economy, gathered by the the Israeli Central Bureau of Statistics. This study centers on the structural conditions that enhanced class structure formation, or, in other words, on the process of the creation of class "in itself" considering the entire class structure in Israel. The two sources are integrated during the presentation of the development of the class structure and the specification of the variables associated with the creation of class positions and the allocation of individuals to these positions. The basic thesis of this study is that, considering the emerging capitalist system everywhere and also in Israel, class "in itself" is unaviodable. However, the process of class formation into class "for itself" and into the center of social cleavage is optional. This is determined by the particular conditions and social agents in the society under investigation.

Thus it is proposed here that the issue of class formation be treated in the "in itself" form. This may be less exciting than a study of politics of class, class struggle, and so forth, but as is contended here, the study of the process of class structure formation—considering the structure as a point of departure—is the proper way to examine the issue of division of labor and the creation of prime conditions that provide the context for consolidation of social categories.

DIVIDED
WE STAND

1

Introduction:
The What and the How of It

Theory in social science concerns identification of the basic social ingredients, the laws of their correspondence, and the conditions in which this is applied to a definite reality. Social theory is intended to deal with the processes that create, maintain, or transfer all or a major part of society. Needless to say, a theory that can elaborate on all these aspects and relate them to the entire society is favorable to one that deals with only one or two elements. Furthermore, theory in a social science is also about the social agents that assume the role of creating, maintaining, or transforming a social structure in whole or in part. Social theory is also used as a directory to select data, as a way of anticipating particular methods, and as a point of departure for certain anticipated outcomes.

This chapter has a modest assignment; it presents the theoretical elements to be used in this book as guidelines for the study of class structure formation, and describes the perspective on class and class formation that is here adopted. It also discusses how this perspective is converted into a study of a sociohistorical period of a certain society. The immediate presentation revolves around the process of class (structure) formation, its correspondence with the major instances of the social formation, and the latter's position vis-à-vis other social processes:

> Class formation is an effect of the totality of struggles in which multiple actors attempt to organize the same people as class members, as collectivities defined in their terms, sometimes simply as members of the society.[1]

In some important aspects, a theory of class structure formation is a derivative of a general theory of social formation. Thus, a perspective on its formation is a "derivation" of the perspective on the latter. The perspective on class and class formation here proposed is of a structuralist nature. This is generally in line with a certain neo-Marxist perspective that is well documented in the literature, let it be said in a few—sometimes competing—versions.[2] There is little need at this point to rehearse either the substance of the controversy or to list the major contesting camps. What is required is first to specify the prime propositions of this perspective, correlating them to the issues of this study, and second to provide an adequate outline (rather than a fully fledged theory) that will be of use in studying the subject of this book. Within the theoretical outlines to be delineated, a number of relevant concepts are incorporated, and, where necessary, given a more extensive explication.

In terms of the present perspective, class is primarily a structural phenomenon. It is engendered in the process of production, or, as some prefer to term it, in the realm of the economy.[3] In effect, engendered class positions are characterized by their innate relations to capital, property, and authority. The product of the latter is a certain composition of class structure that is made possible in the particular society by the particular articulation of mode(s) of production within the social formation.[4] However, this is sufficient to explain neither the process of individual class formation, nor of class structure formation. Class is engendered in the process of production, in other words, in the economic instance of the society, but in other instances such as the political arena, class is formulated, if at all, as a social agent, class-qua-class. Thus, to descend from the theoretical level to concrete reality, one must invoke the propositions that specify: (1) the "relative autonomy" of the political and other noneconomic levels of society, (2) in close connection with this, the possibility of the domination in a conjuncture of nonclass processes of formation and, (3) the distinction between the creation of class in itself, and the formation of class for itself as a potential agent of social maintenance and of social transformation.

There is wide discussion of the first proposition and several authors propose that it is derived neither empirically nor from the Marxian text. In support of their position, it can be stated that there are definite second thoughts about economic determinism. Thus attempts are made to provide more flexible concepts to handle the variety of nonstandard social realities (where the class structure diverges from the anticipated one), and to account for different historical conjunctures under a general heading such as "the transition toward capitalism."[5]

The point is that while exploring the process of class formation, one should consider the relationships between the major instances of the social formation, that is, the matrix in which the former process occurs. If one views the relationships between the economy, politics and, say, ideology, as "modes of determination" as Wright labels them, the following becomes evident: when the process of class formation is examined in a certain social reality, the noneconomic components should be considered in terms of their relative social and historical effects on the formulation of class, and most crucially, in terms of their effects on the economy, in other words, on the primary base for the creation of class positions.[6] It is almost impossible to comprehend a major shift in the composition of the class structure let alone its entire transformation (or even of a certain class) without the effects of noneconomic instances.

The present perspective can be identified as based on the historical "realm of opportunities."[7] The realm of opportunities is a concrete social reality, determine—though not always in-toto—by the "degree of freedom" made available by the economy to the noneconomic instances. This means that in every social conjuncture it must be acknowledged that the limits of the relationships between the economy and noneconomic instances, in terms of certain social processes such as class structure formation, may have one or two effects: determination and/or domination. The structuralist perspective departs from the assumption that the economy determines the degree of freedom of the noneconomic instances, since the former is affected by the latter. Politics, ideology, culture, and so forth do not merely form the super-structure of the economy. They are endowed with the possibility, even if only autonomous to some degree, to influence the social structure or some parts of it, such as reproduction or transformation of relations of production.[8] Simply stated, while politics may indeed be a dominant instance in a conjuncture, it is limited, though not totally determined, by the economy. Hence, political organizations (unions, parties, social movements), while constituting social agents with regard to, for example, class formation, are subject to limits that are set by the economic instance. A substantial change in this respect, particularly social transformation, requires an ascendence of the limits of the economic structure.

The proposition that raises the possibility of domination of social processes other than economics in a certain sociohistorical conjuncture acknowledges the complexity and indeterminacy of the process of class formation, even in capitalist societies. The predominant and singular role of the process of class formation in a capitalist society is presumed, primarily because it is among the few prime determinant components of a capitalist society. Even so, the process of class formation may be accompanied, and also contested, by other processes that attempt to formulate the entire society or part of its institutions in nonclass terms. Thus, in a particular historical conjuncture class formation may be demoted, regressed, or reduced to another process, such as that of a particular ethnic formation, or of nation building, that suppresses other processes.[9]

Which social categories or agents may participate in this competition? The answer is almost every one that is known in social history (ethnicity, religion, class, and so forth). Yet scanning the relevant literature reveals that class formation is related to a particular historical period, that of precapitalist and capitalist formations.[10] This is also highly correlated with certain definite processes, such as nation-state building. This process is most often seen as interpellated with the capitalist era. One predilection equates nation-state building with capitalism in one or another of its stages of development, mainly the transition toward a capi-talist mode of production, in many cases associated with consolidation of the national state.

Nation-state building is a concept used by the interested literature to specify the creation of the nation-state as an independent social entity. Stripped of any specifically sociohistorical content, it can be characterized as a process that incorporates the creation of nationalistic institutions of control and social cohesion, where the state (and state apparatus) constitute a noncontestant institution. The political instance in a state-building conjuncture assumes a dominant position. Hence, the political agents struggle to fulfil the function of creating and maintaining social cohesion, while subjecting any other instance to their ultimate aim. The process of class formation is either demoted, depressed, or utilized to support state building. Nation-state building is then characterized by corresponding limits between the economy and the politics, where political activity endeavors either to establish new degrees of freedom or to subject the economy to political needs and aims by, for instance, applying nationalistic priorities to economic resources and production.

Concrete examples of the above alternatives can be seen in the history of some European countries (for example, the internal unification of Germany or of Italy) and presently in certain countries of central America and Asia. Russia in 1917 provides a lucid historical example of political agents who attempt to control and change the correspondence between the economy and the noneconomic instances, and to subject the economy to political priorities or constraints. The built-in constraints in such cases are certainly demonstrated in these historical ventures and clearly influence their outcomes.

Other competing processes, that in more than one case have taken the lead, are also related, if not contingent, to the process of transformation to a capitalist mode of production. Thus religious formation as a nationwide organization, or ethnic/race formation as a process of establishing distinct organizations within a certain society, can be observed even before capitalism and still accompany it at progressive stages of maturation. In present-day capitalist societies, these are some of the processes that compete, associate with, or cross-cut the process of class formation. It is worth repeating that in certain conditions—to be established by empirical study—these processes may overshadow the process of class formation and even force it to retreat. In other words, the process of class formation is almost never solitary. It is, to borrow a definition from another author, a process of "contested terrain."[11] This is also true for the conditions where class formation is associated with or suppressed by another nonclass agent.

The third proposition offers a distinction between the formation of a class and of class structure. There is a reason to insist on this distinction because of the presumption that the conditions that make class structure possible, in other words, the conditions that are first of all responsible for the emergence of a capitalist system, do not make the formation of a particular class inevitable.

Marx considered the process that engenders class positions responsible for the creation of class in itself.[12] The essence of the present-day denominator of the structuralist perspective is this creation of class positions in the process of production, that is presumed actually to occur in this instance. Thus, the creation of these positions, and their immediate assignment to different locations of ownership and authority, is what class analysis is all about. Class interests, contradictions, and potential conflicts are all deduced from the fact that it is basically the positions in the context of production, and not individuals, that constitute the concrete reality of class and class structure. The core characteristic of the composition of class positions, in other words the class structure, remains firm as long as the predominant mode of production (or the specific articulation of modes) does not change. However, for structural reasons, such as the coexistence of more than one mode of production in a social formation, the boundaries of class may remodeled.[13] Or because of certain technological aspects, the volume of certain class positions in some sectors of the economy may shrink while in others they increase. Essentially, the engendering of class positions is indeed the basic process of class and class structure formation, although it is not necessarily either a linear process or of a fixed form.

The process of class formation is debated in the relevant literature in regard to the consolidation of class organizations, and the possibility of class struggle aimed at achieving class interests. Allocating individuals to class positions is another process offered here. This process is partially independent, but has a strong, innate correlation with the creation of class positions.

The processes that allocate individuals to class positions may be equated to those referred to in terms of "status attainment," a subject much debated in sociological literature, though certainly not embraced by neo-Marxists as a prime process. Nonetheless it is distinguished here, since apart from the political effects on class structure formation that affect allocation to class positions (such as unequal distribution of opportunities based on ethnic origin), some variables of cultural or even personal characteristics may have significant effects on one's chances of being incorporated in a certain class. These include level of education, ethnic origin, country of emigration, and so forth, variables that demonstrate their impact on one's class position through the encounter with the socioeconomic situation, and hence, the "realm of opportunities."

The ultimate aim of this study is to explore the process of class structure formation in Israel from statehood until the mid-1980s. The coexistence of other processes is acknowledged both in the section that portrays the major social matrix parameters during the studied period and in the empirical sections, where certain variables—derived from the parameters—are incorporated in the analysis of the development of the class structure. Because of its centrality during the studied period, the process of nation-state building is reviewed in terms of the creation and development of the parameters of a nationalistic economy and some political organizations. Nation building is the major contestant of class structure formation and is also the most critical process or agent in the formulation of a class structure. As is argued below, nation building was a prime characteristic of the Israeli case.

In one way the economy-cum-social development is presented through the concept of growth. Hence, the major parameters to be noted in this study are immigration, capital inflow, industrialization, reproduction of labor force, distribution of property and income, and distribution of economic power (both political and economic) between the state, the public, the Histadrut (The General Federation of Labor), and the private sectors. These macroparameters were selected a priori because of their assumed relevance to the process of class formation in Israel. They will be used, as will be seen in Chapter 2, to provide the parameters of the socioeconomic matrix of the Israeli society at that studied period.

This study applies a class analysis model to the case of Israel. The class model that is used here is based on Wright's scheme for comparative research.[14] Yet it should be acknowledged from the start that the case of class structure formation in Israel is in certain important aspects historico-specific. Thus, the general propositions should be employed here with some reservation. Israel's basic experience of social history is the transformation from community (under the British mandate) —already characterized by class structure—into state. This society has not experienced the process of transformation from feudalism to capitalism, neither as in Europe, nor even, as in other parts of the globe. Such a transformation had occurred to some degree in the Jewish community in Palestine after World War I. However, the creation of a class structure and the formation of a working class only truly started to develop after the Great War, under the British Mandate. The class structure of the Jewish community was initiated by a process of immigration of Jews to Palestine, first into a semi-prebanded feudal system (the Ottoman government in Palestine until 1917) and later on, into an emerging capitalist system that was predominant in the economy of mandated Palestine, though less so in the politics of the Jewish community.[15]

The general trend that seems to characterize the social history of Israel since 1948 is a process of transition toward capitalism. This process started even before independence; the World War II situation in Palestine encouraged the development of industry, and a labor/exchange market. The process after 1948 was marked by the role of the state in the development of capitalist economy. The features of the process of becoming a capitalist society will be specified with the presentation of the basic parameters of the capitalist development of Israel.

The components contributing most to the process toward capitalism were first immigration of labor and second importation of capital. At the beginning of the 1950s about three-quarters of the Israeli (Jewish) population had been born outside the country. The process of class structure formation was maintained by, and was contingent on, both components. Immigration of labor and importation of capital were the most important factors affecting development and growth, in view of the fact that political institutions of a prestate nature were in existence in almost mature forms before statehood, and took over the political instance after 1948. The process of transition in the entire period placed certain basic limits upon the options that the formation of class structure could have had.

Capital and labor in the nineteenth and twentieth centuries have been migrating to several, mostly capitalist, countries, or those in the process toward capitalism. The concrete manner by which capital and labor were absorbed into the main processes of the country of immigration was determined by the encounter with the particular conditions in the country of immigration. Hence the specific (historical) set of conditions formulated the process and outcomes of the transition to capitalism. This is one of the more fundamental premises of the present perspective. It is thus anticipated here that the process of class structure formation is contingent on the historic socioeconomic matrices of a variety of societies, rather than being of a uniform nature.

Nevertheless, some common rules can be noted concerning basic elements in class structure formation. The most fruitful one, theoretically and practically, is that class structure formation is determined and constrained by the existing and developing realm of opportunities. To this must be added the premise that insists on the effects of the economy as determining the degrees of freedom of the other instances. In the present perspective, these are the minimum necessary premises. A concrete examination of a particular society at a certain time remains open and probably requires elaboration of the stated premises, plus additional ones, such as that which argues for the inverse effects of the noneconomic instances upon the latter.

Chapter 2 presents the basic processes that occurred in Israel from 1948 to the 1980s. Israel was established as a state of immigrants on the very narrow shoulders of an existing social framework. Immigration and state building were intertwined (with a long-standing nationalistic conflict), and the creation of a class structure was inevitable at that conjuncture. Departure from the process of transition toward capitalism is proposed as an essential presentation of the overall processes in Israel during the studied period. Whether or not this was accomplished according to a Western model has no specific importance in this context. The point at issue was whether certain alternatives took precedence over others in the creation and development of the Israeli class structure, that includes both Jews and Arabs. A search for definite information and data was therefore indicated, a methodology adopted in Chapter 3.

NOTES

1. Prezeworski, 1977, pp 372-373.
2. Neo-Marxist literature includes several perspectives such as structuralist or non-structuralist, (such as that of the Frankfurt School). Poulantzas, 1973, 1975; Wright, 1978, 1983, 1985; Althusser and Balibar, 1970; Thompson, 1978; Anderson, 1980. Also for a general discussion see Mayhew, 1980, 1981.
3. Carchedi, 1977; Wright, 1978; Poulantzas, 1973, 1975.
4. Cohen 1978; Wright, 1983; Wolpe 1980; Foster-Carter, 1978, Hindess and Hirst, 1977; Johnson, 1985; Chilcote and Johnson, 1983.
5. Both the supporters and opponents of this conception of structural relationships sometimes share the same general perspective but heavily disagree over both concepts and their correspondence to reality. See, Althusser and Balibar, 1970;

Poulantzas, 1973, 1975; Wright, 1978, 1985; Prezeworski, 1985; Thompson, 1978. These are only examples of the many proponents and critics of the structuralist approach.

6. Wright, 1978, 1985; also, Carchedi, 1977; Poulantzas, 1973, 1975.
7. Prezeworski, 1977, 1985.
8. Wright, 1978.
9. Ben-Porat, 1986.
10. Poulantzas 1973, 1975; Wright, 1978, 1985; also Anderson, 1980.
11. Tilly, 1975; Hobsbawm, 1983; Ben-Porat, 1987; Anderson, 1980; Thompson, 1963; Wright, 1978.
12. Burawoy, 1985.
13. Marx, 1971. The present study deals with the structural aspects of class form-ation, and only includes certain important elements concerning the overall subject of class formation; nothing is said here on the consciousness and organization of class in Israel during the studied period, nor on concrete class struggle at that time. This approach is not exceptional. In 1974 Braverman contended that "no attempt will be made to deal with the modern working class on the level of consciousness, organization, or activities. This is a book about the working class as a class in itself, not as a class for itself." (pp 26-7) Acknowledging the criticism of this approach, however, this study discusses the processes and factors of "class in itself" in Israel.
14. Wright, 1978, 1985, Wright et al., 1982.
15. Ben-Porat, 1986.

2

Israel after Statehood: An Overview

Chapter 1 introduced aspects of the theoretical perspective of this study. It took as a point of departure the realm of opportunities, the structural factors which established the limits to the development and transformation of the class structure of a specific society at a particular period of history. It was established that the particular class structure at a historical conjuncture is also affected by structural but noneconomic factors such as politics, ideology and culture. Whenever the social structure sets limits to the development of a class structure, certain social agents affect these limits. Moreover, in some historical situations structural limits are "imported" to the social formation such as in the processes of colonialism or of nation-state building through mass immigration. The task of Chapter 2 is to identify in greater detail the major factors and conditions that relate theoretical aspects to the "real world," that is, those factors that constitute both the preconditions and the ongoing formulating conditions of class structure. It is thus important to specify the particular conditions and ingredients of the Israeli scene between 1948 and the mid-1980s. Although it is not possible to portray every major event of the period in detail, other writers have presented Israel's sociopolitical history since 1948 with reasonable success.[1] Their writings can therefore serve as supportive background for the present study.

Nonetheless, it is helpful to highlight here some of the major characteristics, and at the risk of some repetition and simplification, to treat these characteristics as major parameters formulating the socioeconomic situation in Israel since its creation as an independent state.

First Israel was and still is an immigrant society. This can be specified as the most important parameter affecting the development of the society. Second, almost from the beginning the Israeli economy was financially assisted by a number of external sources; inflow of capital to the country played an important, even critical, role in the country's development. Third, the Israeli economy underwent structural development from the very start, directing its entire formation toward a capitalist system. The unique process of becoming a capitalist state, despite the so-called socialist regime that was in power until 1977, was exemplified in the structure of society by an increase in industrial enterprises, a redistribution of capital and property, the consolidation of wage labor, the accelerated growth of market mechanisms, and so forth. Industrialization was accomplished by the state as a prime agent while the Histadrut—the General Federation of Labor—and the private sectors were all subjected to the increasing influence of capitalist rules that had dominated the economic level from statehood.

Fourth, politics was the dominant factor in the entire social formation, because the state, in effect the government, exercised major control over the capital flowing in from external sources. In practice this control has fueled the direct involvement of the state in the economy. Indeed, the state has been the predominant agent of "creation" in virtually every sphere since 1948. The influence of this role has somewhat declined, but never to a negligible level.

These seem to be most important characteristics of the Israeli socioeconomic system. Considering the relationships between the Israeli economy and its politics with those of other levels, it can be contended that the class structure of the Israeli society has been heavily affected by the correspondence between the major instances of the society in general and by the state in particular. The government's involvement in the economy is not peculiar to Israel, of course. It is true of most present-day countries, even those that are considered maturely capitalist.[2] However, ownership of property, industry and critical services, and the control of capital inflow have made the concrete role of the state of Israel unique. Thus, the effect of the state in formulating the class structure, although not always conscious, has been overwhelming. Yet even the state acts within structural limits, some of which have been influenced or even initiated by itself, such as the immigration of Jews from certain countries. Other limits have not.

It is worth adding one more point to complete the description of the conditions necessary for class structure formation. The society through the predominant process of nation-state building as well as other processes has been formulated with varying rates of growth. These are divided into three periods that are defined in Chapter 3. The first period was characterized by a high rate of growth in every measure of society that had a distinct effect on the formation of class structure. Thereafter, the growth rates in the major levels of the society were more moderate. Throughout the period the engulfing political situation of the Arab/Israeli conflict had ambient impact on the development of society. This book does not deal directly with this aspect. Yet throughout the following chapters the existence of an external political factor that was responsible in a variety of ways for the structural limits and enhancement of Israeli society is implicitly acknowledged.

Information to be used as a background for specifying the structural conditions—the realm of opportunities—of class formation in Israel follows. The concluding chapter will integrate these background data with information derived from analyzing some of the evidence of the development of class structure in Israel during the studied period.

The background data were taken from various resources, mostly the publications of the Israeli Central Bureau of Statistics (CBS). Where available, the information on the parameters is presented at three points in time: 1961, 1972 and 1983. These years parallel the information on class structure that has been derived from three nationwide surveys, as explained in the next chapter. Occasionally the information covers other years, starting in 1948. Updating information for 1986-87 rounds off the chapter.

IMMIGRATION

Table 2.1 presents gross statistical information on immigrants by major continent of emigration. The information is condensed from the original sources into five-year groups.

Table 2.1. Immigrants by Period of Immigration and Continent of Emigration: 1948-1983

Period of Immigration	Total	Europe and America	Asia and Not Africa	Known
1948-1960	981,227	445,113	515,595	20,519
1961-1971	383,937	183,966	199,701	270
1972-1983	373,128	314,056	59,072	—

Sources: CBS, Statistical Abstracts, various years.

The statistics on immigration since 1948 provide some substance to the above-stated argument on structural limits and rate of social growth. Immigration constituted a critical factor in the development of the socio-economic system of Israel, amounting to more then 1.8 million immigrants in about three and a half decades. This figure is even more impressive when one notes that the Jewish population as of May 1948 was only some 650,000, and the entire population in Israel (including non-Jews) was some 800,000. The labor force was thus based largely on immigration and the impetus for development was motivated, indeed forced, upon society by immigration. The rate of immigration in the first five to ten years, was scarcely comparable to other countries of immigration; about 75% of the population in Israel in the mid-1950s had been born outside the country. The share of immigrants from Asia and Africa is indicative regarding, for example, the quality of the imported labor force. Little effort is needed to derive the limits and the advantages of such a situation.

While Table 2.1 does not provide complementary information on emigration from Israel by recently arrived individuals who considered the country as a transitional stage, or by the Israeli-born immigration and its weakening stream in the 1980s was nonetheless an important factor throughout the studied period.[3] It should be noted that the majority of the immigrants in the 1950s and 1960s possessed no property or capital when they arrived. In the 1950s those who emigrated from Europe were mainly refugees, who after World War II were located in camps for displaced persons in Europe, and had very little opportunity, if at all, to regain their previous status. Only in the mid-1950s did the West German Republic start to pay reparations to individual holocaust survivors, and immigration then became related to capital inflow. Most of the immigrants from Asia and Africa, whose proportion among the total number of immigrants increased and became predominant in the mid-1950s, also arrived without capital or its equivalent and constituted a potential proletariat. Such, indeed, was the fate of many of them, as demonstrated in following chapters.

Yet immigrants did not arrive quite empty-handed. Some of them, mostly from Europe and America, brought with them skills, knowledge and experience in industry, commerce, and administration and science. Provided it could be supported by an encouraging economic and technical context, this was a potential resource, that could be used as an effective source for economic development.

From the very beginning, the import of knowledge, indicated here by education and previous experience in modern/capitalist industry, was differentially distributed among the immigrants. Those who emigrated from capitalist societies (regardless of the specific stage of capitalism in their country of origin) were better equipped with education and experience of modernization. Table 2.2 indicates the assumed advantage or disadvantage of continent of emigration, arranged in accordance with the division of this study into three periods. The number of individuals with a high level of education is specified as a percentage of the ethnic category in the entire population.

The division between Sephardim (those who emigrated from countries in Asia or Africa) and Ashkenazim (those who emigrated from countries in Europe or America) that is presented here and in other places in this book is gross because countries of different levels of socioeconomic development—even of different modes of production—are combined in the same category. However, even this unrefined division is highly informative of the cross-classifications between major ethnic origin and some social or economic characteristics. This holds true for almost the entire period since 1948. The different proportion of levels of education is one factor that benefited the Ashkenazim. Another factor was the distribution of imported occupations. The gross gap over the years has decreased, but as some studies continue to argue, the gap in education is still maintained, and it is considered to be one of the major factors that sustains the ethnic cleavage in Israel and allocates individuals to economic positions.[4]

Table 2.2. Ethnic Distribution of the Jewish Population and Rate of Higher Education: 1961, 1972, 1983 (Percentages)

Year	Continent of Emigration[*]		% Higher Education 13+ Years	
	Asia and Africa	Europe and America	Asia and Africa	Europe and America
1961	42.3	52.1	3.0	12.7
1972	47.4	44.2	5.0	19.3
1983	44.1	40.0	10.0	28.6**

* With addition of Israeli-born second generation not presented here, this totals 100%.
** 1982.
Sources: CBS, Statistical Abstracts; Ben-Porath, 1985.

This has had a distinct effect on the formation of the class structure. There is, as can be seen below, a continuing, almost one-way structural relationship between ethnic origin and the process of allocation to economic positions. Hence the socio-economic level of the country of emigration seems to have a direct effect on one's position in the class structure in Israel. This is obviously a probability based on the ethnic group as the unit of departure, rather then on individual merit. Thus, while taking into account variance within the ethnic group, the probability that an immigrant from a nondeveloped or a semifeudalistic country, will be assigned to the proletariat rather than to the middle class is higher than for immigrants from a developed country of origin. The ethnic effects on class formation have not been systematically examined in Israel. Nevertheless, some studies that delve into ethnic inequality and/or status attainment, provide more than mere clues that a correlation between ethnic origin and class structure (defined in terms of positions in the economy, as explained in the following chapter) has indeed occurred in Israel, probably with varying intensity during the period.

The contribution of immigration to the shaping of the structural conditions of the Israeli society has been well established.[5] At this point some of the internal ingredients of the immigrants should be noted in order to explain in part the difference between the major ethnic group vis-à-vis the labor market, and later, vis-à-vis the class structure.

The first wave of immigrants immediately after statehood in May 1948 consisted of European Jews. Sephardim immigrated in great numbers in 1950-51 and later constituted the majority of the immigrants until the 1970s when the U.S.S.R. became the major source of immigrants. The rate of participation in the labor market was higher among the Ashkenazim because of the age composition in each category, and hence, the number of bread winners in each family. The size of the Ashkenazi family was smaller than that of the Sephardim, but participation in the labor market was higher.[6] One of the reasons was the nonselective immigration policy of the government that encouraged the immigration of big families (essentially of Sephardi origin) with many very young and old people. Although an attempt was made by the government to change this policy in the early 1950s, it quickly revived and thus this attempt had very little effect on the participation of Sephardim in the labor force in the first decade after statehood.

Table 2.3. Occupation before Emigration: 1961, 1972, 1983:
Employed Persons* (Percentages)

Occupation/Year	1961*	1972	1983
Total	100.0	100.0	100.0
Scientific and Academic	8.8	20.0	29.3
Other professional and technical workers	—	21.8	28.4
Managers and clericals	12.3	12.4	17.7
Commerce and Salesmen	15.0	9.1	8.0
Service Workers	2.7	4.5	3.2
Agricultural Workers	4.8	0.4	1.4
Industry, Building and Transport	49.2	31.8	11.4
Others	7.2	—	0.6

Data for 1961 were arranged slightly differently than data for the other years.
* Male earners aged 15 and over.
Sources: CBS Statistical Abstracts

Additional supportive data may be valuable for further identification of the factors that enhanced class structure formation in Israel, such as the distribution of immigrants by their occupations before emigration. In accordance with the earlier arguments with regard to the contribution of the country of emigration to allocation into class position in Israel, this data may add some refinement.

Many immigrants in 1961 (and also in 1972 and 1983) had to change their occupations upon absorption. Sicron reports that from 1948 to 1952, between 50% and 70% of the immigrants in the labor force had to change their occupation.[7] Keeping in mind that the classification of occupations prior to arrival in Israel was based on information given by the immigrants and thus is liable to be biased, this is still an impressive proportion. Very few cases like this are known to have occurred—the United States in the late nineteenth century may be another example of forced change of occupation and class by mass immigration.[8] There is some research and basic statistics provided by the CBS that provide information on subsequent waves of immigration and on the relationships between continent of origin, education and occupational change. It appears that immigrants with lesser qualities had to change their occupations more than others.[9] Some obtained less rewarding occupations in terms of relative earnings than they had before emigration. Immigrants from Asia and Africa underwent more radical changes than immigrants from Europe and America, and the latter had a better "bucket" of occupations in terms of white/ blue collar division prior to their emigration. This seems to have been an advantage for this group upon immigration to Israel. In general, the occupational structure of both Ashkenazi and Sephardi categories grew closer to that of the veteran population in the first decade.

Although changes have also been forced on immigrants in subsequent years, the depth of change remains contingent on the socioeconomic level of the country of emigration and on the encountered level in Israel. With the developing economy of the country and the changing quantity and quality of immigration, occupational change became less radical. The literature on class and on occupation points to a strong, substantive correlation between occupation and class position. Occupational distribution is to some extent an indicator of class structure, although it cannot be used as an alternative explanation.[10]

Hence, by gathering information on occupations and some of their correlates, it is possible to suggest that some individuals are more likely to become proletariat than others. Among the most important factors that determine immigrant occupational (class) change and mobility are those of ethnicity, immigration (here defined as "years in Israel" or "citizen's seniority") and education. As will be developed in subsequent chapters, these factors are also effective in the process of allocation to class positions.

CAPITAL INFLOW

In terms of causal relations, the effects of capital formation, concentration and other effects on the overall growth of a country[11] and on class structure formation,[12] are well documented. The Israeli case is unique due to the coexistence of an accelerated rate of growth and almost no domestic capital formation at all in the first decade, because of the inflow of capital assistance to the state.[13] This situation was largely reproduced in later years when the gross national product was not sufficient to cover the expenditures of the state, or when the foreign debt "by far exceeded" the growth of national product.[14] From 1948 onward the state was engaged in absorbing immigration, developing industry, in manipulating the standard of living of its citizens and in financing the growing expenditure of security. Some analysts point to the dynamics of immigration and economic growth[15] and/or to the rapid increase in productivity and output as explanations of how the state was able to survive through development.[16] The prime explanation, however, should be sought in the stream of capital inflow to the country.

The critical effect of the inflow of capital, partly of a unilateral nature, and partly as low-interest loans or simply as grants is evident when one observes other parameters such as the country's GNP or the national budget. Thus, unilateral capital constitutes 7.2% of the (average) GNP for the years 1952-1955, 5.9% for 1956-1960, and then 13.5% and 13.8% of the GNP for 1976-1980 and 1981-1983 respectively. The critical effect of the import of unilateral capital on the Israeli economy and noneconomic instances is also evidenced by the import surplus, that has fluctuated around 20% of the GNP.[18] Hence long-term borrowing and unilateral transfer of capital have "covered" the deficit for the entire period. Unilateral capital import has accounted for one half to two-thirds of this deficit. Thus the ability of the government to pursue different economic ventures, to influence the standard of living of the population, to maintain a highly equipped army, to colonize the occupied territories, and so forth, was made possible because the genuine Israeli economy was not the only source for capital gains, material products and expenditures. Therefore state politics could be exercised beyond the degrees of freedom set by the country's economic resources.

Table 2.4. Capital Inflow to Israel by Recipients: 1948-1983 (in millions of dollars)

| Period | Total | Recipients | | | |
		Individuals	Institutions	State	Unknown
1948-1955	837.0	81.7	336.0	404.3	15.0
1956-1960	1314.7	440.7	389.6	459.1	25.3
1961-1965	1687.8	1004.2	425.7	257.0	—
1966-1970	2439.1	1358.5	1050.7	29.9	—
1971-1975	7971.6	3220.9	2177.8	2572.9	—
1976-1980	12999.5	4247.9	2341.8	6409.8	—
1981-1983	8910.6	2877.8	1733.2	4299.6	—

Source: CBS, Special Publication no. 767, 1985[17]

In addition, the amount of capital imported to the country during the period was higher than the figures presented in Table 2.4, since loans with lower than the prevailing market interest (which turned them into partial grants for all practical purposes) and capital investment by non-Israelis amounted to about 5% of the entire capital that was imported in the 1950s, and to 15% and 8% in the 1960s and 1970s respectively.[19] With other variables, this is also indicative of the development and consolidation of the genuine economy of Israel. However, from the outset the socioeconomy of Israel was distinguished by high growth rates until the late 1960s (see below) and by being dependent on financial support from outside organizations and states then and now.

Further elaboration on the data in Table 2.4 would be superfluous, but it is none-theless apparent that since the mid-1970s (after the Yom-Kippur war, and the 1975 Israel–Egypt truce) the inflow of unilateral capital from the United States. to Israel has radically increased. Except for the early 1950s, when the transfer of capital to the state's institutions constituted 47% of the entire unilateral capital import, the proportion of capital transfer to the government was around 20% until 1973. It then increased to 38%, to 56.6% in 1983, and 67.9% in 1984. The overwhelming share of United States support is indisputable as is Israeli dependence on it. American political influence on Israel, while discrete for most of the period, has increased correlatively.

As noted above, the unilateral transfer of capital to individuals, some 65% of the entire transfer in the mid-1960s, also includes reparations by the German government to the victims of the Nazi regime. From its commencement in the mid-1950s until the late 1960s this source constituted the major unilateral capital import to Israel (reparations both to individuals and to the state). The concrete results of reparations to individuals on inequality and class structure formation were unavoidable.[20] Reparations from the German government were paid almost exclu-sively to Jews from Europe who endured the atrocities of the Germans in World War II. This capital enabled the recipients to improve their positions in the socio-economy vis-à-vis others and to increase their already existing inequality, which was based on ethnic origin.

Considering the possible effects of an import of capital on the society at large—whether this capital is unilateral or in a form of investment for profit—it can be suggested that such capital may have a substantial effect on social inequality, either between individuals or between certain groups.[21] This also holds true for the specific case of Israel, regarding the state's position in the socioeconomic structure. Thus taking account of the direct or indirect influence of the Israeli government on the import of capital and on its allocation, it is clear that the state had a compelling effect on class structure formation.

This point is taken up below, when the state's primary influence on the economy is discussed.

INDUSTRIALIZATION

The industrialization of Israeli society had already been in motion before statehood, mainly during World War II when the economy was subjected to war prerequisites.[22] The situation after 1948 was, however, totally altered by the major political and economic parameters. It should be recalled that industrialization was associated with two other process, state-building and absorption of immigration. It is suggested here that Israeli industrialization was distinguished by its rapid development and the changes that took place within a very short period, coincident with an almost total lack of domestic material and capital resources. This was therefore a unique process in some aspects, and as is shown later on, constituted a major structural constraint on class structure formation. It is unique because it was a relatively deliberate state policy where the state was also an agent of economic entrepreneurship.

Table 2.5. Selected Indicators of Economy: 1961, 1972, 1983

Indicator/Year		1961	1972	1983
Population (1000's)		2,234	3,172	4,149
Labor force part-				
occupation;	Men	79.0%	68.5%	63.5%
	Women	27.6%	30.8%	36.6%
GNP (1000$)		30.044	78.371	108.609
GNP per capita (1000$)		13.719	24.703	26.431
Foreign debt ($ Mill.)		1.094	5.576	29.826
Inflation rate		6.7%	12.9%	373.8%
% Annual growth of (average)*		1950-1961	1962-1972	1973-1983
Output		11.2	9.7	3.4
Labor		4.3	3.9	1.0
Capital		13.5	8.9	6.0

* Israeli Sheqels, based on 1980 prices.
Sources: CBS, Statistical Abstracts, various years; Ben-Porath,1986; Syrquin, 1986.
(When exact information on above years was not available, the nearest year with information was used.)

Table 2.5 almost speaks for itself. The period from 1948 to the mid-1970s was characterized by growth, albeit at varying rates, substantially different for certain indicators with regard to the three subperiods treated here. Some writers claim that the first period from 1948 to 1960 was characterized by impressive growth; a 10% to 11% increase in output is strong evidence for accelerating development at that time.[23] The next period, 1961 to 1972, embodied a turning point resulting from the political implications of the Six Days War that matured in the mid-1970s. A change occured in the composition of the labor force—a split market in which some (Arab) labor was cheaper than others because of political/cultural discrimination.

In addition, the second and third subperiods were characterized by the growing amount of loans and grants to the government of Israel by the United States, and to some extent increased capital investment, mainly after 1967, in industry and other branches as profit-motivated enterprises.[24] The second period was also specified by the reorganization of the economy and, in practice, of the industrial sector and private services such as more high-tech industries.[25] The third decade, 1972 to the mid-1980s is characterised by stagnation and a slowdown of the economy. The high inflation trend (to over 500% in 1984) was accompanied by a zero, or almost zero, growth rate.[26] As to the possible effects of inflation on class structure, one does not have to make extravagant guesses, and the literature makes some important general conclusions.[27] However, as on other occasions, the particularity of the Israeli system has made a difference. State intervention in the economy and welfare system, the inherited policy of indexation of wages and stocks, the power of the trade unions (the Histadrut), other structural limitations such as the (political) "need" for immigration, and the fear of a brain or a capital drain, have mediated the repercussions of inflation on the individual members of society, and even on the entire class structure.

All in all there was a continual growth in the standard of living of the population over the period; consumption per capita increased threefold from 1950 to the 1980s.[28] Information on the consumption of material assets such as apartments, cars, television sets, telephones and so forth supports the above statement.[29] The overall Israeli standard of living is now comparable with that of some European countries such as Italy and Ireland, although discrepancies have sharpened between such social categories as ethnic origin, Jews vs. non-Jews and so forth. This point will be further discussed when the Israeli class structure is treated, but it appears that the conditions for inequality based on ethnic and class ingredients and the emergence of a structure of classes were assembled during and by the process of nation-state building.

The process of growth/industrialization is portrayed here by a number of economic indicators as suggested by the literature.[30] Thus the definition here is conservative, furnished by information from various sources, mainly the Central Bureau of Statistics. Even so it is possible to discern the process of transition to a capitalist mode of production, considering, of course, the political institutions that supported this transition.

INDUSTRIALIZATION: THE CHANGE IN ECONOMIC POSITIONS

This study elaborates on the political aspects of neither the transitions nor the process of class structure formation. Nor does it treat the cultural and ideological aspects of class formation. Still we should not forget that the process of class structure formation is not totally independent of noneconomic aspects that are embodied in the process of capitalization or industrialization. Thus it is affected by certain aspects of politics (preeminently of state intervention), as it is in many countries under transition towards a capitalist mode or even in a mature stage of capitalism.

Table 2.6 continues with the presentation of background information, and includes distributions of the labor force by the major groups of occupations. In an indirect manner these figures indicate the (potential) creation or extension of positions within the boundaries of the economy that reflect the possible shape of class structure and (individual) class composition.

The most prominent change in occupation position during the period was the decrease in persons employed in agriculture. This is correlated to some increase in industry and building and then a decrease in building and a growth in white-collar occupations such as administration and personal services. The changes point to possible changes in class structure composition and, as is shown later, to the problematic nature of class boundaries. This trend is anticipated in societies under a process of capitalization .

Table 2.6. Employed Persons by Occupation: 1961, 1972, 1983 (Percentages)

Occupation/Year	1961	1972	1983
Total	100.0	100.0	100.0
Professional&Technical	11.7	16.6	23.3
Managers, Administrators & Clericals	13.2	17.5	23.0
Merchants & Salesmen	8.6	8.4	7.8
Agricultural Workers	16.9	8.2	5.0
Transport & Communication	4.6	5.2	3.8
Industrial	28.9	23.4	25.2
Building	3.7	8.6	3.8
Service Workers	12.4	12.1	11.9

Sources: CBS, Statistical Abstracts, various years.

The information on industry in Table 2.7 agrees with the main conclusions of Table 2.6: agriculture shows a substantial downward trend. For economic and political reasons agriculture was intended by the government in the early 1950s to employ about a fifth of the labor force but already in the second decade the percentage employed by this sector was reduced.[31] The reduction of employed persons (positions) in agriculture, the increase in industry, and then the increase in services, point to the concrete changes in the structure of the economy and to the inevitable reorganization of the class structure.

The process of industrialization in Israel, as in many other places, turned on the relationships between the economic and the political instances and on the constant effort of the government to control the allocation of resources, with preferences and objects that more often than not did not fit the real limits of the economic possibilities. Politics in Israel after 1948 had to be changed in order to respond to the new limits of the economy. This was evident, for example, in the reallocation of resources to industry through government policy. The immediate point here is that the state through its apparatus was highly involved in the economy regardless of the formal ownership (Histadrut, private sector). Moreover, the need to industrialize forced the government to support the private sector, virtually resulting in a state-created capitalist class. The practical result was the development of industry and services and a new distribution of occupations, as well as the appearance of some new occupations. The implications for the emerging and consolidating class structure seem obvious; with or without direct intention, the state and the economy codetermined the structural limits for class structure formation.

Table 2.7. Employed Persons by Industry:1961, 1972, 1983 (Percentages)

Industry/Year	1961	1972	1983
Total	100.0	100.0	100.0
Agriculture, Forestry & Fishing	17.1	8.0	5.5
Industry, Crafts & Quarrying	23.8	23.8	22.8
Construction & Public Works	9.1	9.5	6.5
Electricity, Gas & Water	1.8	0.8	1.0
Commerce & Banking	11.9	18.9	22.3
Transportation, Storage & Communication	6.4	7.4	6.5
Government & Public Administration	22.8	24.3	29.5
Personal Services & Entertainment	7.1	7.3	5.8

Sources: CBS; Statistical Abstracts, various years.

In order to substantiate the structural context for the processes of creating and allocating class positions, more information is required. Some of it is available through the three-point distribution of the labor force into different status groups in the labor market, as shown in Table 2.8.

Table 2.8. Employment Status of Persons Employed: 1961, 1972, 1983 (Percentages)

Status /Year	1961	1972	1983
Total	100.0	100.0	100.0
Employees	69.8	75.2	78.6
Employers	18.8*	3.0*	4.2
Self-Employed	—	12.5	9.7
Kibbutz & Cooperative	5.8**	5.7	5.9
Unpaid Family Members	5.6	3.6	1.5

* In 1961 employers, self-employed and cooperative members were assigned to the same category.
** Kibbutz members only.
Sources: CBS, Statistical Abstracts; various years.

As might be expected, in view of information on other countries, the proportion of self-employed people and of employers shows a downward trend, and that of employees, an upward trend.[32] However, modern industry is characterized by extension of positions of management and supervision, and this means that the employee category—the possible working class—should be treated as heterogeneous. One can expect to find in Israel in the second and third decades a relatively complex class structure, partially caused by the increase of the positions of managers and supervisors, and also of various professionals.

THE CONDITIONS OF CLASS STRUCTURE

Before moving on to delineate the development of industry—the assumed core sector of modernization/capitalization—an intermediate summation of the information to this point can be offered, regarding the basic conditions for class structure formation in the period under study.

The critical push to industrialization was apparently political and was correlated to the inflow of mass immigration to the country. The encounter between immigrants, many of whom came from underdeveloped countries, and the existing system in Israel determined the immediate results regarding class structure allocation, that is, the allocation of individuals (immigrants and veterans) into positions in the economy. According to the information on occupational change, it appears that more of the immigrants in the 1950s were also forced to change their positions in the class structure compared to those before emigration. Because of the composition of the labor force in the 1950s, the actual "realm of opportunities" at that time, many Israeli-born people enjoyed an upward mobility and became managers and supervisors.[33] The class structure formation process was partially interpellated with the ethnic factor, mainly because of the encounter between less-developed and relatively more-developed systems,[34] as well as a second factor of seniority in the country that favored the veteran (Jewish) population. The lack of capital forced the state to approach other countries. As for the individual immigrant, the less well-equipped ones were more likely to become proletariat then others. *Cetaris paribus*, the country of origin to some extent determined the fate of the immigrants in Israel; those from the less-developed countries were shunted into lower positions in the class structure. There is certain empirical evidence for this in other chapters of this book, but considering the evidence so far, proletarization and other class-structure related phenomena can be assumed with little risk of speculation.

Some indicators on the growth of industry are provided in Table 2.9.

Table 2.9. Selected Indicators on Industrial Growth: 1961, 1972, 1983

Indicator/Year	1961	1972	1983
Establishments	5,140	6,600	6,499
Employed Persons	143,300	229,700	290,700
% Employed in industry	20.7	25.9	24.0
Gross product (IS mill.)	27.908	77.947	107.733
% of Industrial export in the GNP	16.5	32.7	38.9
Gross Investment (IS mill.)**	21.2	140.0	68,786.0

*   Include labor from the occupied territories.
**   At current money values.
Sources: CBS, Statistical Abstracts, various years; Horowitz, 1972.

The indicators of industrial growth in the above table portray only part of the map of industrialization; more is added by probing the policies of the government of

Israel, particularly its later role in the emergence and consolidation of an indus-
trialist class, that constitutes the core of the capitalist class. Other criteria of
industrial-sector growth over the period in terms of investments, products, exports
and share in the entire economy point to this trend; an increase in the share of
industry, then stabilization and an increase in the share of finance and services.[35]
This was accompanied by a growing trend of concentration of capital within big
companies in the private sector, the government, or Histadrut.

THE STATE IN THE ECONOMY

In the immediate years after statehood Israel lacked most of the prime ingredients of industrialization: sufficient capital, trained labor and entrepreneurs. The
state together with other existing organizations such as the Jewish Agency (an
organization of world Jewry) assumed the roles of entrepreneur and capitalist,
playing a crucial function in the industrialization of the society—sometimes as the
sole agent and sometimes with the cooperation of the Histadrut, public organizations, and individual capitalists. The state because of its position could operate
on a much larger scale than the others. However, the government had to pay com-
mensurate attention to economic and political constraints that affected its policy.

The part played by the state in the economy, and in industrialization in particular, was much more critical in the first decade. But the state continued to be
involved in development of the economy in the subsequent decades. Even in the 1980s
when a capitalist sector has been well developed, and public corporations are more
heavily involved in the economy and in industry, the state is still a dominant agent
in the industrialization of underdeveloped areas, for example, both within the
borders of Israel, and across the "green line" in the occupied territories. Here
industrialization (or lack of it) in the Jewish and Arab sectors respectively, is associated with the politics of occupation.

In the beginning, the government invested more capital in agriculture. This was
intended to increase employment in this sector, while enlarging the number of
agricultural settlements in the less populated areas of the country. Until 1956
industry was considered a second preference vis-à-vis agriculture (and building!). A
change in this policy occurred quite early, yet it was correlated to the capability of
the agricultural sector that had increased its productivity to a surplus.[36] This policy
change directed more capital to industry. Thus 21% of the capital imported to Israel
between 1950 and 1963 was directed to industry, electricity, and mines, 34% to
building, and 17% to agriculture even though the investment in agriculture was still
relatively high.[37] It should be noted that agriculture before 1967 was tied to the
establishment of new settlements, the absorption of immigration and the creation of
an infrastructure. Government policy toward industry improved during the years,
however, and the amount directed to this sector taken from the state budget
increased, while that of agriculture decreased.[38]

Capital was becoming available to private capitalists or corporations through
the special banks that were established by the government or through other

channels backed or guaranteed by the government. Another way to support industrialization was through legislation that encouraged foreign investment. This was followed by regulations to protect industry from competing imports, to provide low-interest loans to industry and lower taxes, and financial incentives for industrial exports.

Industrialization is not an isolated process of emergence and development, nor is it always a continual, semilinear process.[39] It also involves the increase of productivity in agriculture that results from labor saving and capital accumulation. This was, in fact, an important incentive for increasing the state's support to industry. The rapid increase in the productivity of agriculture occurred in a sector already well established in the economy even before statehood;[40] kibbutzim and also "moshavim"—farming communities in which each family owns a farm, but with much of the marketing and other economic activities conducted communally—and private farmers. These prestate bodies were populated by quite highly motivated and enriched human capital, that explains the rapid gains in the agricultural sector after statehood.

The modernization of this sector even preceded that of industry. The increase in productivity in gross measure and per capita freed some labor force, that was then partly directed to industry. The kibbutzim, for example, whose agricultural productivity accelerated very rapidly, established their own industries. Thus industry became a leading, if not exclusive, sector in the economy of the country. The gross product of the country's industry constituted about 25% of the GNP of the entire economy. The status of industry since the mid-1960s is almost incontestable. Following the traditional and conservative definition of industry that is used here, it appears that the development of this sector had already reached a certain ceiling at the beginning of the 1970s. Thereafter, this sector continued to grow in absolute terms, but not so regarding its share in the overall economy.

This section on industrialization is intended to constitute part of the context for the emergence of class structure and of its formation. Yet industrialization epitomizes a larger and more substantial process, the process of transition to a capitalist mode of production. There follow the prime elements of industrialization, essentially those of the process of capitalization. These, however, form only part of the whole process of the development of a capitalist mode of production because the latter centers both on the economy and on noneconomic organizations such as political parties. Nonetheless, it seems that almost no process of the emergence of a capitalist mode of production can be genuine without industrialization. The abundant literature on this issue, which some authors have preferred to call "modernization," suggests a detailed analytical conceptualization.[41] The main elements laid down in the relevant literature are here delineated. The specific articulation of these elements is pursued in the process of transition to capitalism, that in the thesis propounded in this study, has characterized Israeli society.

INDUSTRIALIZATION: A FURTHER LOOK

As is possible to infer elsewhere, the push for industrialization is correlated in a causal manner with the development of the agricultural sector. In fact the technical development of agriculture is in many cases a necessary precondition for the development of industry as an independent sector. For various reasons a stage is reached in agriculture where less labor is required to produce the same amount or even more then before. Moreover, sometimes the more affluent strata of peasants have started to accumulate capital and this capital has been used to start an industrial process.[42] Historical evidence points also to the emergence of an industrial nucleus out of the agricultural sector.[43]

Basically, the ability of agriculture to produce more with less manpower freed labor (and capital) that could be utilized to establish and maintain industrial enterprises. There was a common feature: transformation occurred in a relatively historical continuity, with feudal lords, vassals and peasants undergoing processes of transformation and mobilization, while retaining some other characteristics such as regional or state/country continuity almost intact. Mobilization of labor was enforced, but usually within the existing or reorganizing political and cultural nation-state. The relationships between agriculture and industry in Israel, on the other hand, had ideological/historical connections.

Agriculture in Israel for many years before statehood and during its first decade was entrusted to strongly ideological and political elements. After 1948 agricultural settlements were also used as a political instrument for absorption of immigrants, for the dispersion of population, and for defense purposes, all as integral parts of state policy.

The agricultural sector was (and still is) composed of these components: kibbutzim, private farmers, veteran moshavim (established before 1948), and new moshavim populated by immigrants who had arrived after 1948. Although the first three groups had already achieved high productivity even before statehood they had then to deal with the new level of demand for agricultural products that subsequently resulted from mass immigration.[44] Also, the new moshavim were populated by newcomers with little prior experience in agriculture. However, in a very short period from 1948 to 1956 domestic agriculture was able to provide the growing population with many products, and even produced a surplus.[45] As noted above, this surplus enabled the government to modify the budget priorities in favor of industry. Thus at the end of the 1970s and in the early 1980s the percentage engaged in agriculture—excluding temporary labor, mainly Arabs from the occupied territories—was about 5% or even less. Kibbutzim, whose agricultural productivity reached high levels, turned to industry and became an effective component in this sector.[46]

Yet since the mid-1960s there has been little change in the percentage of persons employed in industry, remaining at about 24.5% of the overall employed labor force. The rate of industrial production in the country's GNP and the rate of export, increased. The most impressive change occurred in gross investment, from 21 IS million in 1961, to 140 IS million in 1972 and 68,786 IS million in 1983 (see Table 2.9).[47]

Industry became more capital intensive. The labor force was mobilized to other sectors, public and private services, that were continually increasing and consuming capital and labor. This is neither a surprising nor a deviant case. Developed societies exhibit a clear trend toward less industry and more nonindustrial enterprises such as services.[48] Israel exhibits this trend in the 1980s, although for reasons different from those in more developed countries.

A correlated effect of industrialization in general is a change in the ingredients and composition of the labor force. First, more females join the labor force. Their distribution curve among the various branches of the economy is assumed to be different from that of males. They tend to be concentrated in public and private services and to be employees rather than employers, self-employed or even managers/supervisors. However in terms of class, females like other minorities in some capitalist societies tend to be overrepresented in the working/proletariat class, as can be deduced from their positions in the occupation and sector distributions and their status in the workplace.

Second, the labor force becomes more educated, and the age of joining the labor market is deferred. Finally, it is expected that during their lives in the labor market individuals will experience more mobility of occupation or of sector of the economy, or both.

The gross data concerning Israel agrees with the above points. The participation of females in the labor market increased from 26% in the mid-1950s to 36% in the early 1980s. This rate differs by age or maternity status. The distribution of females in the economic branches and by occupations has improved during the period. Yet females still occupy positions of lesser authority in the economy vis-à-vis males.

The age of an individual's entrance into the labor market has increased. This can be inferred from the decline of the rate of labor-force participation of men and women (+14), partly because of more schooling, partly due to the extension of military service from two to two and a half years, and then to three years for men. By years and by content, the amount of education of the labor force has improved. The statistics on the educational level of employed persons indicates a considerable change in composition since 1948.[49] The takeoff point occurred when the proportion of more than 13 years of schooling of the employed persons reached over 25% at the end of the 1970s. This fact can be attributed to the improvement in the educational system, the increased participation of more educated females in the labor force, and also to the fact that the average education level of more recent immigrants was higher then before.

Individual mobility in the labor market started almost immediately upon arrival in Israel. As already noted, the proportion of immigrants who had to change either occupation or branch in the economy or both was 60% or more. Some later studies point to the various factors that have encouraged or discouraged mobility in Israeli society.[50] Since these studies treat status attainment as their point of departure, their conclusions can make little contribution to the present study. Nevertheless it is possible to suggest that the structural changes in the economy and politics of Israeli society have had a prime effect on the odds of mobility of various social categories such as gender, ethnicity, and culture.

Industrialization of a society involves capital formation in complementary or even competing ways. Capital formation refers to the accumulation of capital by means of saving and investment.[51] This implies that in certain conditions, such as in an underdeveloped economy with no external financial support, restriction of consumption by individuals or by the government is a necessity. In many "normal" cases the process of capital formation is self-engendered as it is in a capitalist system where domestic profit, saving and so forth are the substance of capital formation. At the very outset of industrialization, investments tend to be concentrated in the emerging industries and certain business services. This is followed by inequality of wages between industry and agriculture, not to mention within industry itself.[52] Also, government enhances a process of accumulation through a designedly discriminatory policy of reallocation of resources through the state budget and so forth.

The rate of domestic saving by the Israeli citizens—which is considered a factor of capital formation—was influenced by what happened to the socioeconomy of society over the years. The import of surplus capital made domestic saving negligible for capital formation.[53] In the first decades the high rate of production growth (around 10% annually) made a significant contribution to domestic capital formation, but could not satisfy the proliferation of social needs. Information on domestic generation of capital points to fluctuations throughout the period; it appears that until 1972, "gross domestic investment exceeded the import of surplus (of investment capital) by a significant margin. But after that year, domestic investment was less than the import surplus."[54] According to this author private savings were on a steady rise from the 1950s to the 1970s. They then began to decline. Government policy had an important effect on this trend.[55]

The data on the basic parameters of the standard of living of the population reaffirm that indeed the income per capita increased as expected in industrial societies.[56] The type of household appliances changed very considerably; for example, 2.4% of the population had refrigerators at home in 1955, and over 90% had them in 1983. Thus industrialization affected almost all the individual members of society, although it had an unequal effect on different ethnic divisions. Also, although the improvement in the standard of living was possible because of the huge inflow of unilateral capital, there are some indicators that Israeli society also became a modern, practically capitalist one because of genuine efforts resulting in an increased level of education of the labor force, an increase in the number of domestic entrepreneurs and the concentration of capital, an increase in the production per capita, and a continual development of highly sophisticated industry and internal and external markets. These efforts are not unrelated to the role of the state in Israel.

THE STATE AS AN AGENT

The function of the state in present-day developed societies is well acknowledged in theory and practice. Yet state support was already recorded at the very beginning of industrialization in such capitalist countries as Japan, Germany and even the United States. In essence, the state played a sometimes indispensible role in enhancing different stages of the process of industrialization.[57] But whether forced to do so or not, it also took care of the distribution of income and sometimes of property that was distorted by industrialization itself. In the light of the Israeli state's heavy involvement in industrialization, it had to consider the consequences and become involved in the redistribution of income, checking the level of inequality in the society.

The state's multiple status as an owner of active economy, political agent, and economic entrepreneur, made it possible—with the unilateral capital inflow—to combine industrialization and welfare in the same governmental organization. The inner contradiction between the two functions was not eliminated, but was often moderated.

In capitalist/democratic countries, state redistribution of income (and sometimes of proprty) is used as an instrument to gain and then maintain the state's legitimacy.[58] This was and still is true in Israel, but has been only one of several factors forcing the state to take a dominant role in the economy. For sociohistorical reasons, the Israeli state had to fulfil the function of both political and economic agent, because no other agent was available in 1948 to deal with the major issues of immigration absorption, security, and so forth.

Immediately after independence there were few potential agents of industrialization. The state, which inherited the British mandate, thus became the owner of public services as well as an owner of key industries (electricity, water, and so forth) and of other enterprises which the original owners could not continue to operate, but which were in some cases essential. The Histadrut was already an owner of components of the economic sector, personal services, health organization, and industry, and constituted a concrete economic entrepreneur, although its resources were limited. The Jewish Agency, a world wide organization, constituted the major independent organization with some capital. This organization was responsible (in cooperation with the state) for immigration and its initial absorption. It was also engaged in the country's economy through the establishment of certain enterprises, mainly where the new immigrants were being settled.

But even the resources of this organization were far less than necessary for an emerging society. The last potential agent might have been the individual capitalist—the genuine agent of industrialization elsewhere—but was initially available neither with effective resources nor in sufficient numbers. Not until the 1960s, was the state able to assume an effective role in encouraging the growth of capitalist entrepreneurs.

The state, the Histadrut and the Jewish Agency had some common denominators from 1948 until 1977 when the government shifted from Labor to the Likud. These organizations were dominated by the leadership of the labor party, first by MAPAI (the Workers' Party In Israel), and later by the MA'ARACH (a federation of MAPAI and other parties of the left). This made it possible for the state to ensure its social and economic policies through the articulation of political parties, trade unions, and in part, individual capitalists.[59] As is shown in Table 2.10 the state and Histadrut employed about 40% of the labor force, and about the same percentage of productivity was and still is attributed to them. Both have constituted a dominant political power since 1948, while individual capitalist organizations that constituted the major share of the economy have been deficient and primarily dependent on the state.

Table 2.10. The Private, Histadrut and State* Sectors: Selected Indicators:
              1961, 1972, 1983 (Percentages)

Decade** Sector & Indicator	1	2	3
Establishments	100	100	100
Private	97.2	97.5	96.4
Histadrut	2.2	2.3	3.3
State	0.6	0.2	0.3
Persons employed	100	100	100
Private	76.0	73.0	66.0
Histadrut	14.0	15.0	18.0
State	10.0	12.0	16.0
Produce	100	100	100
Private	72.0	66.0	54.0
Histadrut	16.0	19.0	22.0
State	12.0	15.0	24.0

*   State refers here to the public sector including the Jewish Agency.
** A decade refers here to the 1960s, the 1970s and the beginning of the 1980s.
Sources: Bergman, 1986; Barkai, 1968; CBS, various publications.

Considering the economy in terms of the sectors shown in Table 2.10, the share of the public sector—state and Histadrut—seems reasonable when compared to other countries, particularly, capitalist ones.[60] This is misleading if one fails to take account of some other facts. The state and the Histadrut—closely related in the first decades—were both owners of various economic enterprises. Hence the state was, and still is, an owner of industry.

But its impact through ownership of some critical industries only accounts for part of the state's involvement in the ongoing activity in the economic sector. The power of the state has been based on the control of a substantial share of the capital in the country, gained as tax revenue on income, corporation taxes, and other indirect forms of tax that the state can use for expenditures. Despite the change in the political-economic regime from an apparently social democratic to the apparently liberal-conservative leadership of the Likud, the place of the state in the economy has remained as before. To illustrate: government expenditure including military expenses as a portion of the GNP amounted to 36% in 1970, 41% in 1975 and 32% in 1982. This is considered a comparatively high expenditure. Taxation as percentage of GNP rose from 35% in the 1960s to 46% in the 1980s.[61]

Thus in practice the Israeli state assumed the predominant entrepreneurial role from the start, mostly through the assistance of other states or organizations in the form of grants, loans and so on. In a direct or indirect manner, but with explicit intent, the government invested public capital in the infrastructure of basic industries. This was the policy until the mid-1950s. Then the government established investment corporations and subsidiaries to support industry and related branches of the economy.[62] At the end of the 1960s the government sold some of its subsidiary companies (such as the shipping company ZIM and the oil refineries) to private investors. This was repeated with some limited success by the new regime after 1977.

Nonetheless, the government never relinquished its control of the economy, which it maintained by control over imported capital in the form of grants or loans, by direct control over the import of foreign currency, by involvement in the stock market, by affecting the pension funds of nongovernment organizations through legislation, by direct export incentives, and, obviously, by its tax policy regarding individuals and corporations. Some of these means of interference in the economy are also used in other countries. However, in the case of Israel this highly intensive interference has affected the development of the entire social structure.

In more then one respect the Israeli state made an attempt to overcome the limits of the economy on the society at large and to become a predominant agent in the process of industrialization, mainly, but not only, because of meager alternatives. In some ways the behavior of the government was a continuation of prestate politics and was affected by ideological bonds, both socialist and nationalist. Its relative success in transcending the limits of the economy was made possible by the high inflow of unilateral capital, loans, and to some extent, profit-seeking investment. Thus because of its sometimes critical influence on the economy since 1948, the government has had a direct, if variable, influence on the creating and maintaining of conditions for class structure formation. Mainly because of its assets including incoming capital, taxes, and industry, the state was able to mold the conditions for a class structure, as well as to moderate, through a welfare policy, the unpleasant consequences.

STATE AND INEQUALITY

Because of the particular situation in Israel after 1948, such as the mass immigration, the lack of domestic capital, and so forth, the government had to take a decisive role in the process and mechanisms of distribution (and redistribution) of property and income. This was effected through income-tax policy, the transfer system that was established by the state, and by other avenues. By affecting income and property distribution the government partly determined the composition of "within-class" boundaries, as well as the boundaries between classes. Moreover, government policy may affect the form of the class structure, allowing certain classes such as the petty bourgeoisie to expand and encouraging the growth of a capitalist class. The following information refers to income distribution. Data on property that are highly important for class analysis at the societal level are scarce.[63]

The information in Table 2.11 refers to the entire population in Israel, Arabs and Jews, (the former constituted from 11% in 1952 to 17-18% in 1986) but excludes Arabs in the occupied territories.

Inequality by Gini coefficient was reduced during the period, although not dramatically. State intervention by means of tax and welfare policy was partly responsible for the level of inequality as well as the above reduction. Alternative sources suggest the same trend with different value of estimates, probably because of differing units of comparison (family–household; per person, and so forth). Some suggest a more dramatic estimation of inequality.[63] A more refined and probably more productive distinction for the present interest can be achieved by inspection of the coefficients for certain subgroups. Thus the difference between employees, the self-employed, and employers in 1984, was almost twice in favor of the latter, an indication of a possible class-based inequality in Israel.[64]

Cetaris paribus, the major contributing factor to social inequality in developing societies is the accelerating process of economic growth and, correlatively, of industrialization.[65] Some categories of people become less advantaged than others because of the objective situation and their capacities. It is possible to moderate this outcome of economic growth to some extent by the intervention of the state, regarding, for example, redistribution of income through a transfer system. The process of industrialization in Israel was characterized by rapid changes in both the structure of the society and the individuals in it. The change in occupation after immigration, the decrease in agriculture vs. the increased volume of industry and services, and the internal changes within the industrial sector toward more sophisticated production signify some of the more prominent structural changes that affected certain individuals and social categories.[66]

Table 2.11. Income Percentage in Deciles of Families by Annual Income
per Household, and a Gini Coefficient: 1963/4, 1972, 1983

	1963/4*	1972	1983
Total	100.0	100.0	100.0
Lower decile	1.5	3.0	2.4
Second decile	3.6	5.0	4.3
Third decile	5.2	6.1	5.5
Fourth decile	6.6	7.1	6.8
Fifth decile	7.9	8.1	8.0
Sixth decile	9.1	9.1	9.4
Seventh decile	10.7	10.6	11.0
Eighth decile	12.8	12.4	13.1
Ninth decile	15.9	15.4	16.1
Upper decile	26.8	23.2	23.4
Gini's equality coefficient	0.36	0.30	0.32

* Information on 1963-64 was the nearest to 1961: information on this year refers to
all urban families while the information on 1972 and 1983 refers to urban families
of employees only.
Source: CBS Statistical Abstracts, various years; Ginor, 1979.

Through the the state budget and using its hold on other resources such as grants
by world Jewry, the government could affect the standard of living of many of the
citizens through direct financial support or through the shaping of the social environment. The state's expenditure on social services, education, health, employment,
housing, income maintenance, and so forth is precisely instrumental for such
purposes. This expenditure amounted to 18.5% of the national budget in the mid-
1970s, and to 25% in the early 1980s, about 20% of the GNP of those years.[67]

In cases such as education or health, government participation reached 85% (education) and 60% (health) of the entire expenditure on these public services in the
1970s and even more in the 1980s.

These and other services, that can considered as potential or real income, had
some definite variable effects on the distribution of income, on the standard of
living, and probably on social mobility. But the point is that government expenditure for social services has influenced inequality in the Israeli society as well as
other governmental activities aimed at moderating gaps between certain social
categories.[68] This exemplifies the real power of the state as well as its limitations.

The Israeli state has been able to influence inequality in society through redis-
tributing expenditure in certain public services and through an income-maintenance
policy. But the state is bound by the amount of disposable resources available at any
period and by the needs of the society, some of which are imposed on the state, and
others are the effects of its policy.

As stated and restated in this chapter the limits on Israeli state expenditure were
less stringent than might have been because of the unilateral capital import and
partly, because of tax policy. Thus the government was able to moderate some of the
inequality in the society. Other factors, mostly related to individual merits in the
labor market, such as education, occupation, age, and length of employment during
the year, were and still are responsible for inequality and explain about half of the
variance in the income of the employee/head of family.[69]

But neither public expenditure nor direct transfer payments for income maintenance could eliminate inequality in income, and/or in property. Definite factors
deduced from the socioeconomic structure may add further, more basic explanations.
In order to explain inequality in an industrial capitalist society, one must take as a
starting point the structural factors that set limits to the capability of individuals
through definite social arrangements and, in essence, to the entire capitalist system.
State power is never unlimited and rarely overcomes the limits of the economy or
other instances. This has been true for Israel despite the fact that it has been able to
spend more than its internal revenue. The welfare policy of the state was, in fact,
contingent to a certain and significant extent on the inflow of capital, mainly from
the United States.

TOWARD A CAPITALIST STATE

The history of Israeli industrialization has been substantially a process of
transition toward a capitalist system, distinguished by the social conditions and
historical specifics of Israel. In fact this process started almost immediately after
World War I, with the British mandate in Palestine and the creation of a
protocapitalist Jewish community with a socialist sector in the still underdeveloped region and semifeudal society. But after 1948 some basic characteristics
had changed. The major agents that had been there before statehood remained after
1948 and were the last to change. But the socioeconomic system was different in both
quantity and quality.

Mass immigration was the key factor for change and later for stability or even a
slowing down of the economy, and of other noneconomic instances. In some critical
aspects this mass immigration was different (nonselective) from pre-1948
immigration. The ratio of immigration to the mean Jewish population was high
even before 1948 (for example 28.3% was added in 1928), but prestate immigration
was different in terms of social motivation, education and family composition.[70]

Capital inflow to the Jewish community in Palestine before 1948 was also massive
and some of it was unilateral as it was after 1948. However, after 1948 the support
from other states vastly exceeded the contribution of Jewish communities abroad and

the former now became crucial as an alternative for capital accumulation, which is a precondition for transition toward capitalism. Although, capitalism was introduced to the Jewish community in Palestine (and also to a certain extent to the Arab community) before statehood, the process ascended to a new level after 1948.

The existence of the state as a factor of cohesion marked a substantive change in the capitalization of Israeli society. The predominant social democratic regime in the government from the 1950s until the mid-1970s was the prime agent in facilitating the development of a capitalist system. This occurred, however, in less than favorable conditions for capitalism building. Lack of domestic capital was a major constraint. On the other hand, the surge of mass immigration within a relatively short period, provided a magnitude of labor that was "untied" economically. The inflow of capital that followed immigration made an advanced restart to the process of capitalization possible. The degree of experience in entrepreneurship that was gained before statehood, and the existence of certain political institutions at the point of statehood, both ignited and maintained a process of state building associated with one of capitalism building.

The view of the process that occurred in Israel as a process of transition toward capitalism makes it possible to suggest a distinction between the most primary structural effects and a set of related effects. A prime structural change is epitomized here by the reorganization of the class structure or the creation of a new class structure. Yet, class structure formation in Israel was embodied in the process of nation-state building that, for sociohistorical reasons dominated any other social process, at least in the first decade.

The process of nation-state building sets up the preconditions for a "class in itself" both for a specific class and for the entire class structure. The distribution of positions in the organization of production and their consolidation in the various industries of the economy, sets up other conditions for their aggregation into class categories. Because of the predominant role of politics in the process of state building it is possible to suggest that under these circumstances politics prove to be effective in forming the basic conditions of class structure creation. Politics, as suggested above, was a predominant instance supporting the emerging process of capitalization. The state was then able to ignore the limits of the country's economy because its power was not bounded by the real capability of the economy. Thus the basic characteristics of the process of industrialization were embodied in the process of transition toward a capitalist system. The mobility from agriculture into industry, the accelerated urbanization, the extending internal market, the increasing influence of the capitalist rules and so forth, specify the major structural changes in Israel ever since statehood.

It is not possible here to establish a causal relationship between state and class structure formation, but the general parameters of state/politics/economy relationships, provide more than mere description. It is possible to suggest that the Israeli state indeed set up some of the more necessary conditions for class structure formation, and correlatively, its reformulation. The interference of the Israeli state in the economy and the role that it fulfilled in the process of class structure formation, both in the formulation of conditions for creation and also in the process of class "for itself," was subjected to limitations as with other states. In order to overcome these limitations, it was necessary to tackle their causes. The state of Israel, because of its unique sociohistoric position, was able to alleviate the immediate limits of the structure, that is, the economy. Moreover it is possible that the process of transition was partly initiated by the state although it was governed by a social democratic (at least by conception) regime. As in similar societies the conditions for class structure and its further formation were an option that had already commenced before 1948, but was still open to alternative routes after statehood.

The end of the first half of the 1980s may be used as a guide to estimate the socioeconomic parameters of the second half of the decade, considering these parameters as the conditions, or at least the main indicators of the conditions, for class development, its maintanance or reorganization. One does not need too much imagination to treat this half of the 1980s, since this book is being written in 1988 and a fair degree of information is already available. Furthermore, even without detailed information on the five-year period in question, it is implausible that the socioeconomic structure could be changed dramatically within such a short time. The class structure is no exception in this matter.

The major parameters regarding the economy and the relevant social institutions seem to suggest that the second half will be almost the same as the first half of the decade. This implies neither that this period is identical to the previous one nor that changes could not occur in the economy or at other levels; indeed some changes have taken place, such as the drastic reduction of the rate of inflation from more than 500% to less than 20% within one year. But this has not changed the basic conditions of class structure.

The economy of Israel in the years between 1984 and 1989 was still characterized by slowdown. The lack of immigration was conspicuous and affected both the economy and politics. Nontheless the quality of the labor force seems to be as good as it was in 1983; more educated individuals (over 29% with +13 years of education), more females have joined the labor market, and positions with relatively high qualifications seem to be increasing. However, the basic composition of occupations, industry and status at the workplace remain as before. Thus the structural parameters of class structure formation have not changed in any radical manner that would justify the possibility of a deep tranformation of the latter.

Some indicative changes have taken place. The percentage of persons employed in public and private services has increased, while those in industry and building have decreased. The number of Arab employees from the occupied territories has increased, (as well as unemployment in the Israeli labor force!) and the Israeli class structure formation continues to be related to this factor of cheap labor, unorganized and available for the least attractive jobs in the Israeli economy. The second half of the 1980s has reenforced the assumption that the formation of the class structure in

Israel after 1967 became contingent on the transformation to Arab labor in the occupied territories and continues to take place both in economic and political terms.

Considering the status of females, individuals from Asia and Africa, and Israeli Arabs, one can point out to a double-effect trend; the absolute position of these categories has improved, but their relative position vis-à-vis males, immigrants from Europe and America, and Jews, remains almost intact. This has implications for the "fate" of these categories in the class structure, that in practice they continue to be an occupants of less attractive positions.

Other major parameters seem to continue the trend from the first half of the 1980s; the inflow of capital, mostly from the United States has increased and still constitutes a most important factor in the socioeconomy of the country. It constitutes about 15% of the GNP. The GNP per person has not improved much, the foreign debt is still higher than in the first half, and the gross investment in the economy and industry is less, both in absolute and in percentage terms, than in the first half of the decade, which, as already pointed out, was far worse than in the 1970s.

Inequality in the Israeli society has increased. The Gini coefficient for 1984-85 was 0.35 as opposed to 0.32 in 1980. The gap between the poor and the rich has widened. It appears that, as before, the most affected were the minority groups, mostly people who were born or whose parents were born in Asia and Africa, and Arabs.

The 1977 change in the political regime did not revolutionalize the state's role in the economy. In fact, the state's position remained almost as before. The second half was influenced by the subsequent political regime (1984-1988) that was a combination of the two major parties in Israel, the Labor alignment and the Likud. In some aspects state involvement increased; because of the state's sole function in the "healing" arrangement adopted as a solution in a major crisis involving nearly all Israeli banks, the state became highly involved, and actually constituted the critical factor in the financial sector. The government started to sell its factories to private ownership, but remained the sole importer of certain goods. The government still controls the massive imported capital to the country, not to mention its allocation. As before, government expenditure constitutes a high proportion of the GNP, and it or the state is the most powerful agent in the country's economy, politics, and other instances.

Thus the estimation of what has happened to the Israeli class structure toward the end of the 1980s is almost straightforward. The relative stability of the major parameters suggests that the the composition of the class structure persisted. What might be happening is that in the intraclass composition there is more internal variety of "statuses" and rewards within the particular class. But in essence the class structure of the mid-1980s seems to be identical to that pictured a few years previously.

NOTES

1. Eisenstad, 1985; Horowitz and Lissak, 1977.
2. O'Connor, 1973. It appears that state interference in the economy is not confined to an unmatured capitalism. Foley, 1978; Reynolds and Smolensky, 1971.
3. Lamdany, 1982.
4. Bahral, 1965; Hanoch, 1961; Hercowitz, 1976; Hartman, 1981, Amir, 1986.
5. For the correlation between immigration and economic growth, see Ben-Porath, 1986. The high number of professionals such as physicians in Israel was an effect of immigration.
6. Sicron, 1957; Patenkin, 1967.
7. Sicron, 1957, also Matras, 1963-64, 1965; Klinov-Malul, 1976; Bonne, 1959.
8. For the United States see Howe, 1976; Handlin, 1973. For Australia, see Evans and Kelley, 1984; also Ben-Porat, 1986-87.
9. Ben-Porath 1986; Matras, 1965; Sicron, 1957; Pack, 1971.
10. Wright, 1978, 1985; Duke and Edgell, 1987. In 1985 Wright published a modification of his basic study on the operation of class structure, but this was only a modification, and not a qualitative change in the basic principles or, more importantly, in the basic assumptions on the concept of class and its derivations.
11. Kuznetz, 1965, 1966.
12. Sweezy, 1942; Poulantzas, 1975; Carchedi, 1977; Braverman, 1974.
13. Horowitz, 1972; Ben-Porath, 1986; Pack, 1971.
14. Barkai, 1987.
15. Ben-Porath, 1986; also on the United States, Etzioni, 1983.
16. Syrquin, 1986; Gaathon, 1971.
17. Shetzer, 1987. See also Razin, 1983. On the various sources of capital inflow to Israel, see Halevi, 1986.
18. Ben-Porath,1986.
19. Shetzer,1987.
20. The effect of reparations on inequality could be discerned by observing the standard of living of certain groups in the population. See also Halevi, 1986.
21. Bronschier, et al., 1978.
22. Horowitz, 1972; Ben-Porath, 1986.
23. Halevi and Klinov-Malul, 1968; Ben-Porath, 1986; also Horowitz, 1972.
24. On the growth of economic investments in the 1970s, see Syrquin, 1986.
25. Ben-Porath, 1986; Halevi and Klinov-Malul, 1968; Klinov-Malul, 1986. See also State of Israel, Labor Force Surveys.
26. Barkai, 1987; Metzer, 1986.
27. Hirst and Goldthorpe, 1978.
28. Ben-Porath, 1986; Barkai, 1987.
29. Ginor, 1979; Syrquin, 1986.

30. Kuznetz, 1965; Satrinati, 1979; Stephens, 1979; Kerr, et al., 1960; Piory and Sobel, 1984; Giddens, 1973; Turner, 1975. As anticipated, the concept of industrialization and the concept of capitalism correlate but only to a point. Marxists do not agree among themselves on the use of these concepts. See for example, Scott, 1979, Chap. 1.

31. Horowitz, 1972; Halevi and Klinov-Malul, 1968.

32. Wright, 1982. See also the compararative study by this and other authors on other countries, Goran, 1981; Goran and Wright, 1983; Singelmann, 1987.

33. This is evident from the various sources of statistical information on labor force and mobility by the CBS and from other fragments of information on this subject. For a more controversial approach to this subject as part of an ethnic base interpretation, see Smoocha, 1978.

34. Taylor and Hudson, 1972, provide comparative information for the 1950s and 1960s. See also Syrquin, 1986; Chenery, et al., 1986; Syrquin, 1984.

35. Halevi and Klinov-Malul, 1968; Ben-Porath, 1986; Barkai, 1986.

36. Barkai, 1983.

37. Horowitz, 1972.

38. Pack, 1971.

39. Piory and Sobel, 1984.

40. Aharoni, 1976; Barkai, 1983. It is assumed in the relevant literature that some definite association between agriculture and industry is required in order to enhance industrialization, yet the exact correlation between the two is debatable. For a more general discussion on modernization or industrialization, see Udy, 1970; Kuznetz, 1955; Aminzade, 1984, and for a different perspective, Brenner, 1976; Stephens, 1979.

41. Kuznetz, 1965; Kerr, et al., 1960; Chenery and Syrquin, 1975.

42. Aminzade, 1984; Brenner, 1976; Tilly, 1975.

43. On the commercialization of farmers/agriculture and the transition toward capitalism, see Hobsbawm, 1969; Thompson, 1963.

44. For performance in agriculture before 1948, see Horowitz, 1972.

45. On agriculture after 1948, see Barkai, 1983; Bernstein and Swirski, 1982.

46. Barkai, 1987.

47. CBS, various years.

48. Ofer, 1967, 1986; Singelman, 1978.

49. Amir, 1986.

50. Matras, et al., 1984; Lewin-Epstein and Semyonov, 1986.

51. Cherney and Syrquin, 1975; Syrquin, 1986.

52. Kuznetz, 1955; Willamson and Lindret, 1980; Jackman, 1975.

53. Halevi and Klinov-Malul, 1968.

54. Mayshar, 1986.

55. Halevi and Klinov-Malul, 1968; Mayshar, 1986.

56. Ginor, 1979; Ben-Porath, 1986.

57. Kerr, et al., 1960; Leachman, 1976; Strinati, 1979; Piory and Sobel, 1984.

58. Offe, 1974; Habermas, 1975. Also on Israel, Sharkansky, 1979.
59. Ben-Porat, 1979; Sewitzer, 1984.
60. Ofer, 1986; Singelman, 1978; Goldthorpe, 1982.
61. Ben-Porath, 1986; Kop, 1985.
62. Aharoni, 1976; Sewitzer 1984.
63. Information on income distribution and on property is derived here from Ginor, 1979; Ben-Porath, 1986, CBS, various years; Yariv, 1984.
64. Even-Shoshan, et al., 1985.
65. Kuznetz, 1955, 1965; Williamson and Lindret, 1980; Wilensky, 1976.
66. Klinov-Malul, 1986.
67. Kop, 1985.
68. Avnimelech, 1974; Achdut, et al., 1979; Kop, 1985; Yitzhaki, 1986.
69. Ginor, 1979.
70. Ben-Porath, 1986.

3

The Present Matter: Class Model and Data

This chapter is intended to serve as a link between the presentations of the major socioeconomic parameters of Israeli society since 1948 which are considered as conditions for the emergence and development of class structure, and the form and content of class structure which is explored in this study. The division of the period into three subperiods is defended; these will be used as three points of comparison concerning the formation of the class structure, referring to the creation and maintenance as well as the transformation of positions in the economy.

The prime source of the data that is used in this study is also introduced. Most importantly, the class structure model is presented and the practical rule by which classes and their boundaries were identified. This chapter is thus mostly concerned with aspects of methodology. Nonetheless, many technical terms that are most often utilized in social research, including (long) elaborations on statistical instruments, are omitted. The relevant reference is pointed out where necessary.

The period that lasted from 1948 to the mid 1980s is divided into three subperiods: 1948-1961, 1961-1972 and 1972-1983. This division was chosen for the practical reason that nation-wide data by the Central Bureau of Statistics in Israel (CBS) is available for three corresponding points of time. Although alternative divisions are possible and may also be effective for the present purpose, the division into the forementioned subperiods has substance in the social history of Israel, and it correlates to the major socioeconomic events which occurred during the overall period.

The first subperiod was characterized by simultaneous supporting and obstructing processes: mass immigration, a moderate inflow of capital, the downward mobility of many immigrants, a relatively high percentage of people in transit camps, accelerating growth, a lower capacity to provide food and shelter, and so forth. The conditions of class structure formation were explicit—such as proletarization enforced on many of the immigrants—but they were still far less than consolidated. The process of creation of class positions was, *ex post facto*, heading the wrong way; at the beginning, immigrants were being directed to agriculture. But the middle of this period was a take-off point for almost every indicator of growth. Considering the alternative conceptualization used here to describe the sociohistorical context of Israel, this growth specifies the early (continuing from the prestate period) stage of transition to capitalism, the early accumulation of imported capital, and the real-location of incoming labor into the sectors of the economy. This was controlled in practice by the state and essentially by the political regime that considered itself to be social democratic as well as an agent of state building.

The second period was characterized by some peaks in growth indicators, by a short recession in 1966-67, and by a critical change in geographic and political terms that resulted from the Six Days War. Immigration to the country became much more moderate than before, but still remained high. Capital import to Israel increased in comparison to the previous period, and most importantly, the composition of the labor force began to change. Arabs from the occupied territories entered the lower ranks of the class structure, constituting a new politically as well as culturally distinct fraction of the working class, distinguished by cultural/nationalistic "boundaries" of noncitizen workers. The ethnic factor became predominant in the political arena, overshadowing any other factor (such as class) in the public debate. Nonetheless, it was highly correlated with the basic ingredients of a class structure. The ethnic collectives were distinguished by their distribution in the positions in the economy, in property possession, and in positions of authority in the labor process. Thus the Sephardic origin was overrepresented in the lower ranks of the economy and underrepresented in positions of power at various levels of the state's political instances.

From about 1972 the major parameters of growth in the Israeli socioeconomic system tended to be downgraded. The Yom Kippur war accelerated this trend. The fact is that by percentage of growth in GNP, investment, immigration, and so forth, the socioeconomic system was now stagnating. The conditions of class structure, such as those related to the distribution of property, income and positions of authority seemed to be becoming more distinct as prime ingredients of class structure. The ethnic factor tended to lose some of its correlation with class, although some ethnic groups continued to be more working-class than others, albeit to a lesser degree than before. Arabs from the occupied territories were now a quite distinct reserve labor force engaged in the less favorable jobs, subjected to other rules than Israeli workers, and without class organization of their own.[1]

The third subperiod incorporated the accelerating deterioration of socioeconomic parameters and then some stagnation until the election of 1984 which ended in a somewhat odd coalition of Labor and Likud in a "national-unity" government. This was aimed at healing the sick economy with a new policy. Whether this had any final success or not is impossible to determine here, though it seems to have achieved certain aims (such as lowering the rate of inflation), but it proved again a general rule: The relative autonomy of the Israeli state was quite effective but only within the limits of the economy, or those limits imposed by external factors, such as United States policy, that are strangers to the politics of Israel

Nonetheless, there are some basic denominators that have shown a continual trend throughout the studied period. The economy continued to grow, although at varying (decreasing) rates. The social institutions such as the political ones were consolidating into a real practical democracy for Israeli citizens. The organizations of the working class, mainly the Histadrut, consolidated their role in a maturing capitalist system and were able to defend and improve the income and standard of living of the employees. This was accomplished mostly by cooperation with the government,[2] but in more than one case also by the use of industrial (class) conflicts at the local and national levels as is shown by labor disputes statistics and other indicators of quasi-class conflict.[3] Until 1977 the regime was dominated by the labor camp or by its various combinations. Then the Likud, a liberal-conservative and right-wing grouping took over. Yet the basic trends of the socioeconomic system remained almost intact and in practical terms the downgrading of the above mentioned parameters just accelerated.

The overall period was also characterized by the competition of ethnic, religious, class, and nationalist agents regarding the formation of Israeli society. The nationalistic factor predominated, constituting a common denominator in almost every individual competition for social formation—state-nation building was the major process of social formation in its own right. Considering again one of the most prominent social competitions (actually conflict) that had different emphases during the period, it appears that the competition between ethnic and class agents over the formation of Israeli society was blurred; ethnicity and class were intertwined in an apparent cleavage between poor Sephardim and rich Ashkenazim, a simple, but false division of class-cum-ethnic combination. Yet, as will be shown later on, the association between ethnic origin and class position was a real phenomenon in Israel and was more complex than the simple division into two categories that cross-cut each other into four possible outcomes only. Public ethnic conflict predominated at certain times during the period, but lost most of its hold in class and in many ways, in political terms in the 1980s. The religious factor, which has, in fact, continued to bedevil Israeli society since the first modern wave of immigration to Palestine in 1882 has some clear cut boundaries such as the many orthodox communities in certain places in Israel. But it has also become interwoven with ethnic and class factors. More than the previous two, this religious factor has been involved in a relentless endeavor to formulate the political-cultural level of the society. In some respects it constitutes a dividing factor giving rise to two camps, the religious in their various communities, and the nonreligious. This division tends to ignore ethnic and class categories.

It should be added here that the present study deals only with the class structure within the boundaries of citizenship, that is, with Israelis—Jews and Arabs. The effect of labor from the occupied territories is not directly treated here. Needless to say, it is acknowledged, as well as the long-standing conflict between Israel, the Palestinians, and the Arab states. The latter had a real, even dominant, influence on the state-building process.

These three subperiods are compared in the following chapters with principal reference to the formation of class structure conditions, the nominal distribution of individuals into class positions in each period, and hence to the process of allocation to class positions. By examining the development of class structure in Israel in each subperiod and by subsequent comparison, one is actually studying the development of a capitalist system in Israel. The capitalist system in Israel is assumed to be different from those in other countries, not in the basic stages of pre- or early capitalization, and matured or developed capitalism, but by the particular correspondence between the economy and the politics in Israel since 1948. Thus the economy is capitalist, being subjected to the basic parameters of this mode of production, but it was and is divided into three sectors: the Histadrut sector (including kibbutzim and other cooperatives), the public/state sector, and private sectors. The share of each has been presented in the previous chapter. All operate according to the principles of a capitalist system, but there are some real differences between them that determine their behavior in the economy and add some unique features to the Israeli capitalist system—the class structure being divided into three distinct pairs of employee-employer positions.[4]

It is thus apparent that while the developing capitalist class did not control the Israeli political institutions, a capitalist system nevertheless flourished. The relationship between government and class organizations, basically cooperative and linked, adds another unique characteristic. It seems therefore that the role of the state in the creation of conditions of class structure in its formulation and reformulation revolved around the development of a capitalist system. To reiterate the argument that was stated above, the state of Israel, for specific sociohistorical reasons, played a crucial role in determining the conditions that encouraged other processes of collective formation beside that of nation-state building. But even the state could not behave as it wished. The subdivision of the period into three categories reflects also the changing relations of limitation and of mutual influence between the major parameters of the Israeli society. This should have had more than some effect on the creation and development of the class structure and the formation of class "for itself."

THE CLASS MODEL

For mostly theoretical reasons, the neo-Marxist controversy centers on the concept of class, while maintaining its original principles. This is associated with the provision of a strategy for researching class structure: its emergence, maintenance and transformation.

In effect the old formula of the class structure in capitalist societies became impractical; a two-class system does not (nor did before) represent these societies' class structure. Those who are concerned with class theory do not hesitate to question its validity when it seems necessary, to reorganize the former concepts and propositions, and then to examine the new or improved theory in an appropriate reality. Hence the contemporary research of class structure by neo-Marxists starts from the concepts and propositions, and continues with variables, indicators, and criteria of class and class boundaries. The point is explicit; class structure is researched as an ontological reality, but class structure in a particular society in a particular conjuncture is treated as a hypothesis, and not as given *a priori*. The class model that is used here is assumed to be subjected to certain structural conditions which, where they exist, enhance the transformation of the class structure.[5]

The class model employed here is that of E. Olin Wright and his associates.[6] This model belongs to the structuralist section of the neo-Marxist school and is based on the following assumptions: first, class structure is determined by the articulation of the mode or modes of production in a social formation. Second, class is first of all an effect of structural conditions. Wright suggests the term "modes of determination" to describe a series of distinct relationships of determination among structural categories of Marxist theory and between those categories and the appearances of empirical investigation.[7] Some definite modes of determination are suggested by this author to explain class structure formation and its derivation from the mode or modes of production that coexist in capitalist societies.[8] This implies that in order to identify the class structure in a certain society, and in order to explain its origin, maintenance ,or transformation, it is necessary to examine class structure within the whole social context. It is therefore also assumed that more than two classes are present in a capitalist society, and besides the two basic classes that reflect the predominant mode of production, the nonbasic ones (the contradictory locations) may be nonnegligible in terms of the rate of positions that they consume.[9] Nonetheless, this assumption should be verified by examining the concrete situation. In other words, while retaining the basic notion of class, it is contended here that the particular social history of a certain society indeed makes a difference in regard to the form and content of class structure.

Although the Wright model draws on a structuralist perspective,[10] its practical definitions of class and most importantly, of class boundaries, are in disagreement with those adhered to by some of the major figures in this school, particularly when the theoretical conceptions of class are decided and then translated into indicators of class structure identification in the real world. The domain of the Wright model refers to the structural determination of class structure, to the distinction between mode of production and social formation, to the recognition of the possibility of more than two classes in the same social formation, and hence to the possibility of a complex class structure that contains classes of different modes of production. Thus besides the other merits of this model it treats class structure in a capitalist system as modular, including standard and also "deviate" classes, those which survive their genuine mode (petty-bourgeoisie) and those that are in a contradicting location.

The research strategy of this model is quite straightforward; class analysis proceeds from the identification of positions in the process of practical engagement in the society's economy. These can be sorted into positions of basic classes, such as proletariat or bourgeoisie—the basic classes in a capitalist system and the positions of contradictory locations. These are "certain positions in the class structure that constitute doubly contradictory locations; they represent positions that are torn between the basic contradictory class relations of capitalist society."[11] These positions in a capitalist society are embodied in managers, supervisors, and semi-autonomous employees (those who enjoy some authority). In both theoretical and practical terms these are not deviating positions; they as much as the basic positions are outcomes of the present capitalist society.

The scheme of a class structure that is portrayed by Wright is as follows:

1. Basic classes within capitalist mode of production: bourgeoisie, proletariat.
2. Contradictory locations within the class structure of capitalist mode of production: managers, supervisors.
3. Basic classes in/within simple commodity mode of production: petty-bourgeoisie.
4. Contradictory locations between petty-bourgeoisie and proletariat (between two different modes): semiautonomous wage earners.
5. Contradictory locations between bourgeoisie and petty-bourgeoisie (between two different modes): small employers.

The criteria that this author uses to assign classes and to draw the lines between classes are: 1. control over the process of investments and accumulation; 2. control over the process of physical means of productionn; and 3. control over the process of labor power of others. In other words, these criteria are based on possession, domination, and autonomy. Basic classes within the capitalist mode of production are antagonized by each of these processes. Capitalists control all three processes, and the proletariat, none. Contradictory locations have an incomplete pattern of control. They either exercise control over one or two of the processes (for example, the petty-bourgeoisie), or they exercise partial control regarding certain processes (managers), but never assume the last stage of this position that takes complete control. Supervisors are employees with some control over the labor process. Self-employed persons control investment, property and so forth, but do not control the labor power of others. Eventually positions in contradictory locations are indeterminant by their relations to basic classes, and to the prime "ingredients" of class (property, authority and so on). In this case politics, ideology, and such noneconomic factors, may assume a critical function regarding the process of class formation and in particular, the formation of class as "class for itself," for example, the formation of a (certain) contradictory class as a component in a coalition of classes with one of the basic classes of the predominant mode of production. While the basic class positions are well documented in the literature, the contradictory locations need more explanation.

The contradictory locations between proletariat and the bourgeoisie are explained thus: "The contradictory quality of a particular location within class relations is a variable rather than an all-or-nothing characteristic; certain positions can be thought of as occupying a contradictory location around the boundary of the proletariat, others as occupying a contradictory location around the boundary of the bourgeois."[12] The range of these contradictory locations may be quite wide ,from top managers in a corporation to first-line supervisors. The former seem closer to the bourgeoisie, the latter to the proletariat. Yet this is determined by the specific political, cultural and other aspects in a certain society, that is, its institutions, specifically ethnic or religious in composition, or stage in capitalist development. In some places managers have shares of the enterprise, and thus they benefit from both wages and profits. In others they do not. In some places supervisors are treated as an integral part of management and in some they are probably closer to the workers' class according to the objective situation of their location(s).

Contradictory locations exist between petty-bourgeoisie and other basic classes, bourgeoisie or proletariat. This refers to locations that are between two different modes of production. Here Wright identifies two typical categories of contradictory locations: small employers and employees. Small employers who employ others (the petty-bourgeoisie does not appropriate surplus value through exploitation of others) could be former petty-bourgeoisie or workers. The small employer who employs very few others is far less than an *haute* capitalist, but the point centers here on the labor relation, not the size or volume of capital or labor. "Where a petty-bourgeois producer employs a single helper, there is an immediate change in the social relations of production for the labor of the worker can be now exploited."[13]

The other category of contradictory locations, the one that is situated between petty-bourgeoisie and the proletariat (the semiautonomous), refers to employees, "who have a certain degree of control over their own immediate conditions of work."[14] Wright suggests that considering the entire capitalist system, it is worth separating this category because, "they control how they do their work and have at least some control over what they produce."[15] Thus, concerning the criteria of class and class structure, this category is distinguished from other workers by certain qualitative variables. Moreover, it appears that this is not a negligible or waning category.[16] Wright himself is not quite sure what the real fate of this category is, being content to state, "It remains to be shown whether the net effect of (these) two tendencies—the expansion of white-collar employment and the proletarization of white-collar work—has increased or decreased the contradictory locations between the working class and the petty bourgeoise."[17]

A study of United States class structure, part of a comparative project on class structure and class consciousness, shows that it contains, by percentage of people in class positions: bourgeoisie—1.8%; managers and supervisors—29.6%; working class—46.3%; small employers—6.0%; semiautonomous—9.5%; and petty-bourgeoisie—6.8%.[18] Class structure distribution in other countries such as Sweden is similar to that of the United States with, however, some differences that are attributed to the sociospecific conditions of the country under study.[19] The general picture of class distribution in Israel (see below) is not very different from that of the above-described matured capitalist states. Some of the disparity is caused by real differences in social structure, and some is caused by the practical definition of the classes in the Israeli study. This similarity is of interest, and if it is not the result of the practical definition, then some more explanation is needed.

In a recent 1985 publication Wright revised his model of class structure. It is now based on the concept of exploitation and of skill and organizational assets. The revised model has an effect on the distribution of classes, mostly on the boundaries; some positions have been moved from one class to another, and the class structure has become somewhat more refined. Nonetheless, it is still the same class structure as regards theoretical conception; it is still based on a structuralist perspective in which one pursues the distribution of positions before counting people in definite classes. It remains based on basic classes and contradictory-location classes, and concomitantly, on the notion of mode of production, the sociohistorical features of this mode, and the option of more than one mode within the same social formation. However the latest version of the model is based on the shift from domination as a criterion for class identification to exploitation. The typology of class location in a capitalist society is based on owners of means of production vs. nonowners, on organizational assets and on skill/creditational assets. This produces twelve class categories of the class structure in capitalist societies (Wright, 1985) that can, however, be reduced in numbers without violating the basic concepts that guide the class structure identification.

The present study, the main characteristics of which are presented in the following section, follows Wright's earlier model. However, although in conceptual principles and in some practical definitions, it is close to that of Wright, it is not identical, mainly because of some differences between the present view of the operations of class structure and the view used by Wright. Following the latter, it divides the class structure into basic classes and contradictory-location classes. But the information used here to construct the class structure at three different points of time since 1948 is limited. The social surveys (see below) that were used do indeed contain data relevant to the typology necessary to construct a class structure of basic and contradictory classes. But these data do not contain a full inventory of appropriate indicators. It was possible using these data to identify the bourgeoisie class as Wright did, and also the proletariat, but managers and professionals had to be combined into one class without the ability to distinguish between managers with credentials and experts with some authority, as suggested by Wright's later model (1985). The problem of who is really occupying a semiautonomous position was also encountered in this study, but because of the nature of the data, the problem was defined in very broad terms. This should affect the boundaries between proletariat and semiautonomous workers and thus the estimation of the size of the working class in Israel since 1948.

As is shown below and in subsequent chapters the problem of the operational definition of class positions through the surveys used here has more than some influence on the comparison between Israel and other countries. But this seems less problematic when the comparison is made within Israeli society over the three periods. It is suggested that the difference(s) in class structure from 1948 to 1961, to 1972, and to 1983 are the effects of real changes in the structure of society, and not just a mere misplacing of positions in the class structure within the wrong region or boundary(ies).

The construction of a class structure for Israeli society since 1948 is based on the information gathered by the Israeli Central Bureau of Statistics (CBS). This government-run organization conducted three general surveys of the entire Israeli population, in 1961, in 1972, and in 1983, respectively. Each survey was designed to examine several parameters of the population in such a way as would make it comparable to the next and/or previous survey(s). Using standard questionnaires, the CBS gained information on employment, place of work, status at work ,and so forth. These items could be used to construct a position of class and a class structure following the basic parameters of the above-mentioned model. This basic procedure is used here.

The surveys were used as the prime source of information for the construction of a class structure for each subperiod. In 1961 and in 1983 the surveys asked about the employment and work of the interviewee before the current employment. In 1961 this question referred to employment before immigration, and in 1983, to employment five years before the time of the survey. The information of employment before immigration had to be treated with some wariness, but was useful for certain purposes.[20] Most importantly, it could be used to explore the immigrant's class position in the country of origin, before emigration.

The CBS used a standardized questionnaire in every survey. The questionnaires of 1972 and 1983 were almost identical, and the CBS used the same coding system for both.

The 1961 questionnaire was somewhat different, primarily in the categorization of occupations into main and secondary groups.[21] This happens to be a minor problem, since in 1972 the CBS issued a manual that provided instructions on how to adjust the classification of 1961 to that of 1972.

The information that was collected by the surveys regarding variables that could be considered as most relevant for class analysis, is in some details different from the variables constructed by Wright and his colleagues in their comparative project. But as presented below, it was possible to construct a practical scheme of class structure which was close to theirs in its parameters and shares the same concepts and assumptions as well as some practical indicators of class.

For the particular purpose of the present study three separate samples were drawn, one from each survey. Each sample contained 7000 individuals. Using the sample technique of the SPSS manual, all samples were drawn from the general surveyed population in Israel, Jews and Arabs, males, and females over the age of twenty-one. The age limit for sample selection of individuals was decided on because of the length of army service in Israel. This study deals with class structure of the Israeli society through the distribution of the labor force, and hence soldiers under compulsory service had to be excluded. The decision to select these samples has the following drawbacks: First, only employed individuals are sorted into classes, and no information is given here on the class position of those not in the labor force. This mainly affects females, individuals in army service, students and retired persons. Second, this affects the Arab population. Israeli Arabs are not required to serve in the army, and they enter the labor market earlier than their comparative Jewish age group. It is therefore important to note that the estimation of the distribution of certain subpopulations into the class structure that is used in this study may be biased. For some of the parameters in this study, this estimation has certain negative effects, but for further analysis, such as by regression model, it may have only a negligible effect. The following outcomes of the analysis should therefore be treated with some caution, although it is assumed that no serious harm is caused to the study.

The class model adjusted to Israeli society was constructed by the use of two items (questions) in the above-mentioned surveys. One is the occupation of the respondent, and the other is his status at his place of work at the time of the survey. Occupation was classified by the CBS into ten major categories, and then into subcategories (secondary and so on) according to the international code for the classification of occupations. The ten major classification groups are ordered in a certain hierarchy according to an assumed status order, from professionals through semiprofessionals, white-collar occupations, and then skilled and nonskilled manual occupations. In terms of division of these into white- vs. blue-collar occupations the order seems proper, although in other terms it is dubious.

Classification of the population surveyed into occupations was accomplished by the CBS. The classification into ten major groups was the "bottom line." For any further analysis of this data, a more refined classification of occupation into secondary and even further classification is available, but is not relevant to this study.

To start with the construction of class frame, the classification into ten major groups was rearranged into this scheme:

Class 1. High-grade professionals, high grade administrators etc.

Class 2. Lower-grade professionals and managers in industry and services.

Class 3. Lower-rank managers, administrators and other white-collar persons.

Class 4. Technicians, skilled workers ,and so forth.

Class 5. Nonskilled employees in industry and other branches of the economy. At this stage of class structure building, the fifth class also includes the self-employed in lower prestige occupations (taxi drivers, vendors, etc.).

The division of the occupations into these five groups follows Golthorpe's scheme in several respects,[22] and the first stage of class scheme building tends to be close to the Weberian notion of class. The above division clusters classes by their proximity to authority and other rewards that specify and mark the lines between classes as a status category. The adding of the next variable turned this scheme into a neo-Marxist form.

Status at the work of place was/is classified by the CBS into the following categories: 1. employer of three or more employees; 2. employer of one or two employees; 3. self-employed with no employees; 4. employee; 5. member of cooperative or kibbutz member; 6. unpaid family member in family business.

This classification is distinguished by category 5. Cooperative members refers to individuals who are members of producing cooperatives (about 1% in the 1980s). They are both owners and employees of these cooperatives and sometimes even employ others. Kibbutz member refers to every individual in the kibbutz (in the present study only people over twenty-one). Less than 4% of the overall population in 1983 were kibbutz members.

The class scheme of this study is based on the cross-classification of occupation groups as the above with status at the place of work.

After rearrangement these classes were produced following the Wright model:

Class 1: The bourgeoisie. This includes employers of three or more employees. The CBS general classification did not provide a more refined division. However, this cutoff point has also been used by others in other countries.[23] While it seems quite arbitrary, it is not far from what is proved statistically to be the share of capitalists in a capitalist society. The problematic point here is with the concrete definition of capitalists in Israel, if and when the number of employees is used as the only criterion. The existence of state-owned industry, of Histadrut industry, and a mixed ownership between the latter and the private sector makes it difficult to tie position (that is identified here through individuals) to class. It is possible that within the category of employers of three and more individuals, one may find managers of state or Histadrut enterprises. As much as the CBS was aware of this bias and tried to take account of it, such cases are possible.

Class 2: Small employers (one or two employees), the self-employed without employees, and unpaid family members. This class is therefore a combination of a basic class position of a different mode of production, that is, the petty-bourgeoisie, and a contradictory location class of small employers in a capitalist mode of production. Members of a family employed in the family business were assigned here since they seem close to a petty-bourgeois position, and are so named.

Class 3: Professionals in high positions who are employees and employed managers in high positions. These are "contradictory" class locations. Professionals were assigned by Wright (1985) to a class category of "experts" who are distinguished in the workplace by credentials typically required in occupations that endow them with power/control over the work process. This is also a contradictory class location. The managers and professionals in this class category are employees in the private and public sectors of the Israeli economy. This characteristic was not distinguished when assigning individuals to this class.

Class 4: Similar (but not identical) to Wright's semiautonomous class and includes skilled workers, lower-ranked supervisors, technicians and other employees who use some kind of expertise (at a lower level than the experts in Class 3) in the work process. First-line supervisors are also included in this class. This is far less than desired in defining this class, particularly because of its already-known problematic position in theory, but it is the "best fit" considering the nature of the data that is used here.

Class 5: The proletariat. This class includes all employees with no control over capital, the labor, or work processes. Both this class and Class 4 can be considered as a working class, but the fact that it is the genuine proletariat working class with Class 4 indicates a possible heterogenity within the working class category.

Class 6: Members of cooperatives and kibbutzim. This category of class is distinguished here for a very substantive reason: it contains individuals in positions that fully integrate both labor and capital. The members of cooperatives and kibbutzim are simultaneously the owners and the employees in the organization. Cooperative organizations also employ hired persons who are not members and thus the cooperative members also employ others. (However, not every producing cooperative employs nonmembers as salaried workers). In principle the kibbutz organization does not employ others but many kibbutzim in fact do so. In one respect this class is a highly contradicted one; it assumes a capitalist position as a collective, and that of the working class or self -employed, as individuals.

This constitutes the sixfold class scheme constructed for this study. The same scheme was adjusted to every survey sample. In practice only individuals in the labor force at the time of the survey were assigned to a class category.

Before proceeding to the program of this study, two elements should be elucidated. First, the threefold division of the Israeli economy into public, Histadrut, and private sectors makes some difference when class positions are assigned. The bourgeoisie in this study is identified here as a position whose occupants employ three or more persons, but when this refers to Histadrut or public-government establishments, the situation is different. In these cases the owner is a political organization, institution, or state. The ongoing operation of these establishments is in the hands of appointed or elected managements and sometimes in state-owned enterprises, of a board of directors. In the Histadrut case the political regime (elected by the mass of Histadrut members) is also responsible for the entire Histadrut economy, and the appointees control investment, labor and work processes. This makes them a substitute for a direct ownership. In the present assignment of positions into classes, the Histadrut's managers and those in the state enterprises, are assigned to Class 3, a contradictory position that appears appropriate in this particular case. In principle this is the same assignment given to managers in private enterprises. The Histadrut managers' class position is thus much more complex than private sector or even state enterprise managers. The former by a formal nexus are also the owners of their enterprises as are the workers—members in the Histadrut's enterprises.

In this study the sector of ownership of the economy is ignored mainly because of the problem of deriving the information on sector assignment through these surveys. But it seems to prove the point that despite the general rules that specify transition to capitalism and those of the capitalist mode as such, each society may exhibit the historic specificity of its structure and the effect of the latter on class structure formation.

In addition, the class model by Wright is based on the contention that more than one mode of production can exist in the same social formation. The two modes that are incorporated in theWright scheme are the capitalist and precapitalist (simple commodity) modes. The modes incorporated in Israeli social formation are the capitalist, Histadrut, and kibbutz/socialist modes of production as well as the petty-bourgeoisie.[24] The kibbutz/socialist mode is assumed to be an embodiment of a future mode of production that, some argue, succeeds the capitalist mode.[25] The truth of this is not the immediate interest of this study, however, and for practical and theoretical reasons, the kibbutz and cooperative class is not treated any further than its identification and proportion in the class structure.

The following chapters discuss the class structure through the presentation of descriptive distributions and their structural correlation with other factors such as ethnicity, culture, gender, and so on. Then the analysis moves on to estimation of certain regression-type models in order to assess the contribution of definite factors on class assignment. That is, it attempts to unfold the process of allocation to class positions. The analysis also includes an estimation of the factors responsible for the proletarization of immigrants and nonimmigrants during the studied period. The process of creation of class positions is treated through the decomposition of class and industrial sectors and corresponds to the previously stated arguments about the structural factors that formulate class structure.

It may seem that this study follows the traditional method of a positivist school, that is, leaning on quantitative analysis of observed phenomena. In defense of this possibly self-defamatory statement, it should be noted that a mere quantitative analysis is not equivalent to a positivist approach. Neo-Marxist study uses quantitative measures in various instances as a direct reflection of the class structure or as proximate indicators of a concept or variable that can not be estimated directly. The disagreement between non-Marxist and Marxist sociology and especially that which takes after structuralism, is about the presumptions regarding social systems and history—what creates, maintains and transfers social organization. This study wishes to be no different than many others that depart from the structure of society in order to identify the factors that determine the realm of opportunity.

NOTES

1. Lewin-Epstein and Semyonov, 1986; Ben-Porath, 1986.
2. Ben-Porat, 1979.
3. Institute for Economic and Social Research, 1964, 1985.
4. Aharoni, 1979; Barkai, 1984; Halevi and Klinov-Malul, 1968; Kleinman, 1987.
5. Wright, 1978, 1985; Carchedi, 1977; Poulantzas, 1975.
6. Wright, 1978; Wright et al., 1982. This conceptual model and to some extent the research associated with it have drawn much criticism. See Giddens, 1985; Carter, 1986; Rose and Gordon, 1986; Crompton and Mann, 1986. The author is of the opinion that the merits of this model still overcome its drawbacks. Actually, one's obligation is to the conceptual model. Class operations may be modified to suit certain situations in differing societies.
7. Wright, 1978.
8. Wright, 1978.
9. Wright, 1978; also Wright, 1985, with this author's modifications.
10. For example, Poulantzas, 1973. The structuralist perspective is no longer homogeneous, but still contains basic principles that distinguish it from other perspectives. Wright, 1980; Mayhew, 1980 and 1981.
11. Wright, 1978.
12. Wright, 1978.
13. Wright, 1978.
14. Wright, 1978.
15. Wright, 1978.
16. Wright et al., 1982. The literature on the self-employed and on the petty-bourgeoisie (contradictory locations within and between modes) is equivocal regarding the fate of this class. See Toivonen, 1987; Becker, 1984: Cuneo, 1984; Singelman, 1978; Dale, 1986; Wright, 1985. On Israel, see Ben-Porath, 1986a.
17. Wright, 1978.
18. Wright et al., 1982; Goran, 1981; Goran and Wright, 1983.
19. Goran, 1981; Goran and Wright, 1983.
20. Sicron, 1957. The information on class position before immigration is based here on the self-report by individuals in the various surveys. Some people tend to report a better position than is the truth. Moreover, some of the immigrants reported on their employment or occupation before World War II, which had not necessarily been the same as that prior to immigration. This is more probable regarding immigrants from Europe than others.
21. The CBS classified occupations according the international code system. In 1972 the CBS modified the classification of occupation and provided a manual to "translate" the new classification into the previous (1961) one. This has been used here for the creation of comparative units criteria of class for 1961, 1972 and 1983.
22. Goldthorpe, 1980.

23. Wright, 1978; Wright et al., 1982.
24. Ben-Porat, (forthcoming).
25. Wright, 1983.

4

The Portrait of Class Structure

> It was not surprising that these aspects of the subject should have received earliest treatment. Towns that suddenly grew into cities and found themselves engulfed in slums. ... The governmental system that swiftly changed under the control of voters with new conceptions of politics. ... These were practical problems in the face of which there was no forgetting the importance of immigration.[1]

Beyond every other factor immigration to Israel in the first decade after independence specified the unique condition of Israeli society at that time. The relevant literature cited in the preceeding chapters suggests that immigration acted as an igniter; it encouraged the creation and the development of other factors and critically contributed to the process which changed the class structure of Israel. The host society of May 1948 was already a class society with a small capitalist sector, petty-bourgeoisie, and a highly organized working class that dominated the political institutions of the prestate society and had important influence on its economy. The change which occurred after May 1948 was both quantitative and qualitative. The numbers were of critical importance; on the consumption side it was necessary to supply the newcomers with certain minimum basic necessities. On the production side the economy was small scale and could neither provide immediate employment nor expand its structure in the short run. Also, it could not meet the increased demand for products.

However, the quantitative aspect was only one face of the problem of absorption of immigration into the economy of the society. The qualitative aspects were no less critical. It should be recalled that by level of education, experience in industry or other modern systems, and by age composition and so forth, many of the newcomers lacked appropriate attributes to meet the immediate situation. Or, vice-versa, the host society was not an appropriate one in this regard. The problem of absorption of immigrants by direct allocation into slots in the economy was practically impossible. Thus during the first few years many immigrants were forced to stay in transition camps outside the labor force and hence, in class terms, in a "declassed" situation.[2] These were unemployed persons by "state permissiveness." At about the same time many immigrants were mobilized by the state agencies into sectors of the economy and regions that the state wished to develop, and thus the class position of these people was determined for them first by the fact of immigration, and second by the situation and policy in Israel at time of immigration.

In 1961, the year in which the first survey was conducted, the situation had changed from the early 1950s. Unemployment was low[3] and many new settlements had been established making the absorption of immigrants into the agricultural sector possible. Without a conscious design the state agency set up grounds for the creation of self-employed, and later on, small-employer, class fractions. With respect to other classes, the "middle-class" in Israel or, the petty-bourgeoisie, was also encouraged by the government. Not intended as a *class structure* policy by the state, it was encouraged for such instrumental reasons as initiating the growth of entrepreneurship. As already argued, state-building formation had a substantive effect on class-structure formation.

The information which is summarized below in Table 4.1 is, as expected, only a partial exploration and presentation of the formation of the class structure through three decades of independence. But it does reflect the major structural changes that occurred during the period; the mass immigration and its entrance into the positions of production in the economy, the changes in the qualifications of the class positions and their redistribution, and the end result of all of these—the formation of a class structure.

Table 4.1. Class Structure: The Entire Population; 1961, 1972, 1983* (Percentages)

Class/year	1961	1972	1983
Total	100.0	100.0	100.0
Bourgeoisie	1.5	1.7	1.8
Petty-bourgeoisie	20.5	18.3	11.4
Managers	14.4	18.6	24.7
Semiautonomous	17.2	22.9	29.1
Proletariat	39.4	32.6	27.7
Kibbutz-cooperative	7.0	5.9	5.3

* With the rest of the following tables, this is based on the three samples, excluding the non participants in the labor force.

The proper way to evaluate the outcomes of the three different distributions over the whole studied period is by introducing the theory that projects these variables in the first place. As is expected from a society in transition toward a capitalist system, the bourgeoisie or capitalists constitute a minor fraction in terms of positions in the economy, but may be an overwhelming one in the possession of capital. This can be and indeed was validated in part by various data on income distribution and property distribution. The proletariat constitutes the relatively major portion of the positions in the process of production, and because of the method used here, these positions are reflected in the distribution of employed persons. These two basic classes agree with the general presumption of a predominant mode and its class structure. This is as expected in a country which undergoes a process of becoming capitalist, however with the particular specifications of that country.

The proportion of the bourgeoisie did not change much during the period from 1961 to 1983. About 1.5% to 1.8% of the positions belonged to this class. Now, as already sanctioned above, these positions are established through public opinion surveys. While the basic ingredients of these positions are indeed explored here, some are not. Positions of ownership and of authority are also interwoven with sectors, that is, government enterprises, Histadrut enterprises and/or private corporations. One should therefore bear in mind that some positions of the bourgeoisie, because of the power assigned to them to invest capital and to manipulate labor power and labor processes, are not reported here through a survey of individuals. They are referred to as "collective positions" in a capitalist or semicapitalist system, and their rate is determined by the strength of certain nonprivate sectors in the country's economy. These positions may be occupied by managers or other nominees of boards of directors and may not be counted in the bourgeois class because of improper report by their occupants. Nonetheless, the particular characteristics of these positions are effects of the structure, such as the correspondence between politics and economy which produces working-class economic organizations (the Histadrut), and not simply of improper subjective reporting or miscounting of position.[4] The managers/professionals class category is therefore much more problematic as regards the real combination of control over ownership and labor, and it is named here, as elsewhere, a contradictory class location within the capitalist mode of production.[5]

The substantial increase of the share of managers and professionals in the class structure, from about 14% in 1961 to about 25% in 1983, can be attributed to the increase in the industrial and the service (public and personal) sectors, and correlatively, to the changes that occurred in the internal composition of industry and services regarding technology, management and the level of required expertise. The internal reorganization of these sectors inevitably affects the division of labor in authority terms. More managers are needed, and there is an extension of the function of knowledge which encourages the demand for more professionals. The increase of this class category is also an outcome of the improving composition of immigration, the amelioration of shortcomings in the educational system and its more even spread within the different social categories of population than in the first decade.

What seems to be the major change is the reduction of the share of the working-class during the three periods. This class constituted a relative majority in 1961 and also in 1972, but not any more in 1983, as it was reduced by about 30% from 1961 to 1983. In simple terms, the proletariat ceased to constitute a relative majority in the 1980s.

This should be reconsidered, however, by reference to the semiautonomous class over the same period. This class of skilled technicians and others is highly sensitive to changes in the structure of the economy. Changes in the economy may provide more semiautonomous positions and more mobility to individuals who had been located in the proletariat and who by additional training could become semiskilled or technicians. This refers to individuals or to their children. Yet a reverse process may also occur; recession adversely affects the opportunities of mobility and can cause downward mobility, that is, a reduction of semiautonomous positions in the economy. Throughout the period, except for 1966-67, the economy encouraged the increase of this class position and consequently the decrease of the proletariat proper.

In 1961 the two classes together comprised more than 56% of the class structure members, remaining almost the same in 1972 and 1983, but with the place of the proletariat now being taken over by the semiautonomous, who became the relatively major class of the 1980s. Considering the possible error in the present sample, the difference of 1.4% between proletariat and semiautonomous may be negligible (Table 4.1), but still the change from 1961 to 1983 in the power of the proletariat vs. the semiautonomous class (a basic vs. a contradictory class) is clearer, to a greater extent than any other change in the class structure from 1948.

It is of much interest, regarding the assumed factors which formulate the class structure in Israel, to trace the fate of the petty-bourgeoisie, a class which survived despite prophecies of its downfall in capitalist societies.[6] The change in the share of this class in the class structure is obvious, going down from over 20% in 1961 to about 11% in 1983, a reduction of nearly 50%. The explanation of the size of this class in the 1960s and its subsequent shrinking (but still surviving) in a significant percentage departs from immigration and moves to major changes that took place in Israel after 1967. In the first decade immigrants became or remained petty-bour-geoisie after immigration because of the meager economic situation at that time. For some this was the only possibility because of age and/or lack of qualifications. Some of those who were directed to agriculture withdrew and moved to the cities where they joined the proletariat or the petty-bourgeoisie. These are the two classes where no formal qualifications are needed for entrance. Their size shrank following the changes in the economy. The new generation which entered the labor market in the 1970s had more opportunities for mobility and better qualifications to exploit the new realm of possibilties.

The 1967 war changed the composition of the labor force in Israel; there now existed accessible reserve labor which was cheap, unskilled, and nonorganized. This made it possible for some Israelis to maintain their positions as petty-bourgeoisie and small employers through the use of this labor. It involved old and new small employers who were, in fact, performing some functional activity in the economy. But the fate of this class seems clear, going down from 18.3% in 1972 to 11.4% in 1983, a reduction of about 40%. It is possible that because of the political changes after 1967 some Israelis were "saved" from becoming proletariat by being prevented from downgrading, or by becaming semiautonomous. The effect of a "split-labor market", based on a cultural/national division, was becoming evident.[7]

The share of the kibbutz/cooperative class was reduced from 7% to 5.3%. This can be validated through other sources that show that the kibbutz in Israel was about 4% of the entire population in 1983, but over 6% in the early 1950s. Table 4.2 presents the class structure in Israel excluding that of the kibbutz/cooperative, and from now on this is used as the basis for comparison and further analysis.

What had appeared at the beginning of the period as an abnormality regarding a process of allocation of mass immigration into class positions readjusted itself during the period into a normal class structure in a capitalist society, with the particular features of the Israeli society. The distribution of classes by positions in Israel in the 1980s is not very different from that of the United States where, Wright reports, capitalists constituted 1.8% in 1982, the working-class between 35.2% and 56.7% (a range from minimum to maximum estimations), the petty-bourgeoisie constituted 6.8%, small employers 6.0%, managers and advisors, 16.8% and supervisors plus the semiautonomous, 22.3%.[8]

Table 4.2. Class Structure: The Entire Population Excluding Kibbutzim/Cooperatives; 1961, 1972, 1983 (Percentages)

Class/year	1961	1972	1983
Total	100.0	100.0	100.0
Bourgeoisie	1.6	1.8	1.9
Petty-bourgeoisie	22.1	19.5	12.0
Managers-Professionals	15.5	19.8	26.1
Semiautonomous	18.4	24.3	30.7
Proletariat	42.4	34.6	29.3

The difference between the distribution of individuals into class positions in the Israeli class structure and that of the United States may be attributed to several causes. First, it may be affected by the mere fact that actual measurement is of individuals who report on their positions, which may have some effect on accuracy of reporting the proper position. It is here suggested that this has had a minimal effect on the results both in Israel and in the United States It may, however, have some effect on the real number of class positions. It is probable that in the present study more than few positions are ignored because of the way the survey counted occupations, jobs, places in organizations, and so forth. Most importantly, the sampling limits used here excluded young individuals who in the United States are active members in the labor force, but in Israel serve in the Army. Moreover, the portion of the labor force employed by the (regular) Israeli Army is not specified here. One can regard the class position of a high-ranking officer and of a Sergeant-Major as belonging to the same sector—state employees—but still to different classes, in regard, for example, to their command of the labor and organizational processes in the army.

The composition of Israeli society vs. that of America may provide further explanation. Some positions in the economy are "enclaves" and are not reported through official statistics, surveys, and so forth. It is possible, however, that the differences in class-position distribution into definite classes in Israel and the United States are the results of concrete differences in the structure of these two societies. The United States is a matured capitalist society and Israel is not. The United States is an advanced capitalist country that is undergoing a transformation from goods-producing industries to service industries.[9] The big waves of immigration to the United States occurred at the end of the nineteenth century and the beginning of the twentieth century, while in Israel this occurred in the 1950s and continued to the beginning of the 1970s, with major effects on the structure of society. The following is a comparison of the general class categories, using Wright's best estimates from his and his colleagues' 1982 publications and the Israeli class structure in 1983—excluding the kibbutz/cooperatives. It seemed that in Israel the bourgeoisie amounted to 1.9% while in the United States it was 1.8%. The petty-bourgeoisie was 12%, and 6.8% in the United States managers/professionals, 26.1% in Israel, and 29.3% in the United States. Semiautonomous, 30.7% and 16.6% and proletariat 29.3% and 46.3%, respectively. The difference is mainly attributed to the practical definition used in the present study, but some results from the structure of both countries. This is also evident in the next comparison.

In Wright's new 1985 version the distribution of classes (adjusted to the present scheme) is: bourgeoisie, 1.8%, petty-bourgeoisie (and small employers), 12.9%, managers/professionals 29.8%, semiautonomous, 15.6% and proletariat, 39.9%.

The use of some different criteria and the gross adjustment of one set to the other is responsible for the similarity (as well as the dissimilarity) of the results in the United States' and Israeli studies. However, this comparison raises a further question. If the previous section specifies some of the assumed causes for the difference(s) between the two societies, it is now more important to ask about the similarities that seem to strike the innocent observer. How can they be explained? In addition, when the small-employers class category, which Wright et al. distinguished, is added to the petty-bourgeoisie, as is done in the Israeli study, the similarity increases, excluding the lower two classes, semiautonomous and proletariat/working.

It is possible to point to various explanations, starting with the fact that Israel is, in economic terms, a satellite of the United States, but because of political reasons it is not subjected to the same economic/political effects of dependency, such as being exploited by big corporations, forced to specialize in certain niches of the world economy, and so forth. While this contention may be provable, it cannot be established here.

A further explanation may lie in the constitution of the economy in each of the two countries. The share of the state in the economy is one factor. In Israel the government employs about 20% of the labor force. In the United States it is close to 22%, including federal and state governments. This means that for a relative portion of the population in both countries their class positions are determined by the influence of the state on the economy and through this influence on the creation of class positions and their allocation. But in Israel the state possesses real, active, economic enterprises run by the state or through subsidiary bodies. In Israel the trade unions (Histadrut) possess a substantive portion of the economy via such enterprises as a major bank, and some public services. This should have made a difference in the class structures of the United States and Israel. In effect, while there is a difference, the present research does not reveal it, probably for technical reasons, as noted at the end of the book.

Hence by a simple comparison of both class structures it can be seen that the Israeli class structure is very close to the capitalist one. Thus the structure anticipated in theory seems to have materialized, though obviously not precisely as anticipated. A further comparison of the class structure in Israel in the 1980s to that of other capitalistic societies such as Sweden or Germany, reaffirms that the general laws of transition toward capitalism are accompanied and modified by the specificity of the social history of every country under this process.[10] Israel is no exception; its class structure is that of a capitalist society in general, affected by Israeli conditions.

A rough division between those who employ another or others, or work for themselves, and those who work for somebody else shows that at least 80% of the labor force in Israel in the 1980s belongs to the the latter category (compared to over 70% of the labor force belonging to this category in 1961). This does not make the latter proletarian; the proportion of semiautonomous employees increased during the period, which may reflect the structural change(s) in the socioeconomic base that reversed the process of proletarization. More skilled employees and more technicians seem to have been required by industry and services. The proportion of the real proletariat (no property, no control over labor process, no authority, and so forth) shrank to about a third of the labor force. The question here is, who gained and who lost by the seemimgly accelerating process of mobility during the studied period? That is, what nonclass social categories, if any, benefited by the structural changes? Who belong to the capitalist class, who to the proletariat, and so forth? The basic source of data that is utilized in this study makes it possible to treat a few selective factors (following the items in the CBS surveys) as direct indicators of certain social categories. Most of these factors can be used to deepen the discussion on the process of allocation of individuals into class-positions, though only one or two can be used to reflect the structural ingredients of the process of class positions creation. The next set of tables deals with class-cum-other social characteristics. This is presented as an extension of the class portrait. As happens with portraits, extra details of only part of the real phenomenon that is pictured are provided at this juncture, while some of the rest will be treated in other chapters.

Table 4.3. Class Structure by Gender; 1961, 1972, 1983 (Percentages)

Year		1961			1972			1983	
Gender and Class*	F	M	Total	F	M	Total	F	M	Total
Bourgeoise	1.9	98.1	100	1.7	98.3	100	7.8	92.2	100
Petty-bourgeoisie	19.0	81.0	100	19.9	80.1	100	18.8	81.2	100
Managers	39.4	60.6	100	39.9	60.1	100	42.8	57.2	100
Semiautonomous	31.7	68.3	100	44.8	55.2	100	54.3	45.7	100
Proletariat	18.8	81.2	100	18.1	81.9	100	21.8	78.2	100

* F = female; M = male

Table 4.3 classifies class and gender for every single period when the class composition is the point of departure. The fate of the men and women over the whole period as class members (or as becoming members) is treated later on in this chapter. According to the class division that is used here, the class composition seemingly changed regarding its gender composition; the share of women in capitalist positions increased in 1983, as did their share in Class 3 (managers, professionals, high-ranking administrators) and in Class 4. In practice, the female share in every class increased. This correlates with the increase of women in the labor market since 1961. The percentage of women in the labor market out of the total category of women was 27.3% in 1960, 31.3% in 1973, and 36.6% in 1983.[11] According to the CBS the female category in the work force has a higher proportion of employees than the male category; about 85% of women in the labor force were employees in 1983, compared to 75% of men in the same period.

In this study individual members of the labor force are assigned directly to a class category. This means, among other things, that gender is treated here only when it is directly associated with class positions. Women (and men) who are not members of the labor force are not assigned here to class position in any other way, although it is possible to assign spouses through their partners' class positions.[12] At this junction class composition is the point of interest, yet it is worth presenting another angle of cross classification to deal with what happened to women compared to men, in class terms, during the overall period.

Table 4.4. Class Distribution of Women and Men: 1961, 1972, 1983 (Percentages)

Class*			1	2	3	4	5
Year and Gender**							
1961	F	100.0	0.1	17.4	25.4	24.1	33.0
	M	100.0	2.1	23.6	12.4	16.6	45.3
1972	F	100.0	0.1	13.4	27.2	37.7	21.6
	M	100.0	2.5	21.9	16.7	18.9	40.0
1983	F	100.0	0.4	6.2	30.5	45.5	17.4
	M	100.0	2.7	15.4	23.6	22.1	36.2

*   Classes as in previous table.
**   Categories as in previous table.

Although this study is concerned with the process of allocation to class positions only as a secondary interest, it is noted here and will be further referred to in succeeding chapters. The distribution in Table 4.4 merely touches on the issue of gender and class since other factors such as ethnic origin and nationality are not controlled. Thus apparently obvious interpretations should be restricted. Arab women, for example, are very different from Jewish ones in their positions in the labor market,[13] and there still are differences between ethnic groups in Israel which influence class structure composition. All these have more than some influence on the distribution of women and men. It would nevertheless seem that women's class mobility was mainly toward Classes 3 and 4. In other words, the female labor force has become concentrated in the contradictory locations. The concentration of this category in these classes can be explained by the factors that determined the development of the economy in Israel and by the changes that took place within this gender category, such as the raising of the level of education.[14] Nonetheless, men still hold most of the positions in the capitalist class, the petty-bourgeoisie and managers/professionals. This is similar to the situation in other capitalist countries in the 1980s.[15]

Table 4.5 presents the distributions of class by ethnic origin, and thus excludes Arabs. It is a standard procedure in the Israeli literature to divide Jews into two major groups; Sephardim—those who emigrated from countries in Asia and Africa, and Ashkenazim—those who emigrated from European countries or from the United

States, Canada, or South and Central America. During the years these categories were also subdivided into those born abroad or those born in Israel but whose parents (mainly fathers) were born abroad. This division is far less then perfect. It might be argued, for example, that a division into two gross ethnic categories is ineffective in explaining one's fate in the class system in Israel. The socioeconomy of the particular country of emigration is much more productive in this matter.[16] This study uses the two general categories as stated above because they offer a good indication and also because of the lack of better information regarding immigrants' positions in the class structure before emigration.

Table 4.5. Class Structure by Ethnic Origin: Jews; 1961, 1972, 1983 (Percentages)

Period and Ethnic category *	1961			1972			1983		
	Seph.	Others	Tot.	Seph	Others	Tot.	Seph	Others	Tot.
Class:									
Bourgeoisie	6.3	93.7	100	27.6	72.4	100	29.7	70.3	100
Petty-Bourgeoisie	18.9	81.1	100	30.7	69.3	100	43.4	56.6	100
Managers and Professionals	11.0	89.0	100	15.7	84.3	100	26.7	73.3	100
Semiautonomous	21.1	78.9	100	33.6	66.4	100	44.3	55.7	100
Proletariat	41.2	58.8	100	51.8	48.2	100	52.3	47.7	100

* Seph = Sephardim, Others = Ashkenazim + Israel-born. Ashkenazim constituted more than 80% of this category in almost every case.

The theoretical background to this study specifies the realm of possibilities of competing processes of social formation with respect to the same people (see Chapter 1). It is therefore important in this section of the study to examine carefully the other potential possibilities of social formation besides that of class, which are the result of certain structural factors and their changes in Israel. Ethnic origin in Israel is one such possibility of social formation which may compete with, or even contradict, the process of class structure formation. Table 4.5 shows that the ethnic composition of class structure changed, and knowing the waves of immigration that entered Israel since 1948, the effects of origin on class structure can be seen to have been substantive. The changes by class are as follows: The bourgeoisie were and remained mainly Ashkenazi and constituted more than 80% of the "Others" category in most cases. The proportion of Sephardim increased but not to a degree that challenged the Ashkenazi majority. The petty-bourgeoisie became more Sephardi during the period, from about 19% in 1961 to about 43% in the 1980s. This class position probably was used as an alternative avenue of mobility by many Sephardi individuals. To become a petty-bourgeois one needs less formal credits, and thus this class that is still part of the capitalist system is still alive in Israel as in other capitalist societies. The improved share of Sephardim in this class can be confirmed by other sources.[17] The Sephardim fared less well in Class 3, their share of which is even less in the 1980s than in Classes 1 and 2.

Class 4 includes many Sephardim whose share increased from 1961 to 1983. Ever since 1961 the proletariat has been essentially Sephardi, whose proportion has grown from 41% in 1961 (the same percentage as the Ashkenazim) to 52% in the 1980s. As will be shown in later chapters, the process of proletarization had a greater effect on Sephardim than on Ashkenazim. More precisely, it had a greater affect on those who emigrated from lower rather than higher socioeconomic levels, *cetaris paribus*, because class before emigration also had some substantive effects on the individual's chance of becoming proletarian.

As with the previous class-related factors, the ethnic distribution by class is also presented in Table 4.6.

Table 4.6. Ethnic Category by Class: 1961, 1972, 1983 (Percentages)

Period and Ethnic category*	1961 Seph	Others	1972 Seph	Others	1983 Seph	Others
Class Total:	100.0	100.0	100.0	100.0	100.0	100.0
Bourgeoisie	0.4	2.2	1.4	2.1	1.3	2.4
Petty-Bourgeoisie	15.0	26.2	16.7	21.4	12.6	11.7
Managers and Professionals	6.6	17.8	8.7	27.9	16.7	32.9
Semiautonomous	14.0	20.0	23.0	26.5	32.6	28.9
Proletariat	64.0	33.8	50.2	22.1	36.8	24.1

* Ethnic categories as in Table 4.5.

For demographic reasons such as the fact that among the Sephardim there was in 1961 a higher percentage of young children, Ashkenazi participation in the labor force was higher.[18] Other factors such as level of education and gender explain the changes in the labor force participation during the entire period as well as the allocation and shifts in class positions. The under- or overrepresentation of Sephardim in the fivefold class structure derives from changes that took place in Israeli society as well as within this ethnic category. In 1983 they were underrepresented in the capitalist class (41.6% in the labor force vs. 29.7% in this class) and also in the managers/professionals class. They were overrepresented in the petty-bourgeois, semiautonomous and proletarian classes where they held a majority. However, the correlation between class position and ethnic origin was apparently weakening during the period, although it still exists.

Another category reviewed briefly here is that of the Israeli-born, not separately presented in the above tables. This category had been located in higher class positions in 1961 (20.8% of this category were petty-bourgeoisie, 21% were managers/professionals), lost some of its advantaged positions in 1972 becoming almost predominantly proletarian, and then in 1983 was predominantly located in Classes 3 and 4 (65%, more then ever before, and comparatively, more than any of the other ethnic category). Thus the Israeli-born tend to became a "middle class" and similarly to women, tend to be located in contradictory locations. This and the previous information suggest that contradictory locations may be a substantive position in the Israeli class structure. This seems true also in more developed capitalist societies, such as the United States, and raises a question regarding the difference between developing and already developed capitalist societies, and their resultant class structures. Together with other relevant points that will emerge, this element will be dealt with in the concluding chapter.

The distribution of the Israeli-born in the three periods may bear some sampling errors, but this should affect only a small proportion of the results in Table 4.6. It is possible that this category indicates the future class structure in Israeli if no dramatic change occurs; a decrease of the proletariat among the Israelis and an increase of contradictory locations classes, which are named, according to the tendency in some of the literature, the middle or new-middle classes. However, regarding the present political situation in Israel, and in particular the existence of a labor reservoir in the occupied territories, it is not possible to reach a definite conclusion from the present distribution of class positions and their comparison to other capitalist societies regarding the development of class structure in Israel. Additional information on the effect of noncitizen Arabs and their impact on Israeli society is undecisive as regards the possibilities at the end of the 1980s.[19] One point is obvious; it is difficult to deal with the class structure of the Israeli society without considering the effect of this last category. However, the present study does not deal with noncitizen Arabs, and it is thus admitted that the description here is lacking.

Table 4.7 presents class distribution by religious and nationalistic factors. Arabs in Israel are citizens, but they differ by religion, certain cultural aspects, and by nationality, a category that is formally distinguished in Israel, although the various religious groups belong to the same citizenry. In the following, Moslems (about 80% of the non-Jews) and others are combined under the religious category of Arabs.

Table 4.7. Class Structure by Religion: Jews and Arabs; 1961, 1972, 1983
(Percentages)

Year Religion	Total	1961		1972		1983	
		Jews	Arabs	Jews	Arabs	Jews	Arabs
Bourgeoisie	100.0	100.0	—	96.4	3.6	96.9	3.1
Petty-bourg.	100.0	90.6	9.4	92.2	7.8	90.7	9.3
Managers	100.0	98.0	2.0	98.0	2.0	93.9	6.1
Semiaut.	100.0	98.0	2.0	96.6	3.6	94.4	5.6
Proleta.	100.0	92.1	7.9	89.4	10.6	80.2	19.8

The non-Jewish labor force amounted to about 6% of the whole in 1961, and to 11% in 1983. In the early 1950s there were concrete barriers to the participation of Arabs in the Jewish sector. They were subjected to military government. This changed in the 1960s. It seems that the most dramatic change in the Arab labor force was their increase within the proletariat. Table 4.8 provides information on the Arab distribution in class positions vs. that of the Jews.

Table 4.8. Distribution by Religion by Class: 1961, 1972, 1983 (Percentages)

Year Religion	1961		1972		1983	
	Jews	Arabs	Jews	Arabs	Jews	Arabs
Class	100.0	100.0	100.0	100.0	100.0	100.0
Bourgeoisie	1.7	—	1.9	1.2	2.0	0.8
Petty-Bourgeoisie	21.3	36.0	19.1	24.0	12.2	10.3
Managers	16.2	3.2	20.7	6.4	27.3	14.3
Semiaut.	19.2	4.0	25.3	11.7	32.3	13.5
Proletariat	41.0	56.8	33.0	56.7	26.2	61.1

In the 1960s Arabs indeed entered the Jewish sector and this fact had an effect on both categories. About half of the Arabs in the labor force was engaged in this sector. During the years more Arabs became "commuting proletariat."[20] This became the most prominent change in the Arab class structure since 1948. Arab capitalists have been few and have probably employed almost all Arab labor. Israeli Arabs are engaged in two different markets, Jewish and Arab, and while the barriers are not strict, the move is almost totally one way, from agriculture in the Arab sector to the bottom of the Jewish economy in terms of occupation and industry. The Arab distribution in the class structure of the entire society and the creation of class positions within their sector are both highly dependent on the Jewish sector for employment and on the state for investments and the extension of the Arab sector.

The level of education of the Arab labor force improved, though far less than that of the Jews. This explains the increase in the semiautonomous class and managers/professionals class. It is argued by some that the effects of the transformation of the non-Jews was more rapid than that of the Jews.[21] The upward class mobility (more precisely, an occupational mobility within class) of Israeli Arabs was enhanced by the entry of Arabs from the occupied territories into the Israeli labor market. These became the "new-appendix" proletariat, but as shown in Table 4.7, the Israeli-Arab proletariat continued to grow in the 1980s.

Beside the cross-classification of class with gender, ethnic origin, religion, and education, year of immigration, age, and sector were also cross-classified. Sector is treated elsewhere, when the factors of class-creation positions are extensively surveyed. As for education, year of immigration, and age, they are presented in a dichotomous manner in Table 4.9, with the rest of the class ingredients which are included as descriptive parameters of the class structure.

These ingredients explicitly indicate the potential adversaries process of class structure formation—ethnic, nationalistic, religious, and so forth—processes which, as already noted, compete with class structure formation, or even cause its subordination. Nonclass properties such as gender, ethnic origin and even seniority of immigration are handled by the sociological literature in various ways; some treat them as prime reasons for the stratification of the social system, and others as epiphenomena of more basic properties that cause them to be shaped in a definite manner.

There is another reason for the treatment of these ingredients here; it is suggested in this study that it is important to make a distinction between two processes that coexist in the same social structure and are related in a structural manner to class-structure formation—a process of the creation of positions of class, and a process of allocation of individuals to these positions. Ingredients including gender, ethnic origin, education, and year of immigration center on the process of allocation. Research concerning this process has flourished in recent decades and provides some account of the contribution of these properties to the division of statuses and to the consolidation of stratification systems.[22] No less important is the contribution of these properties to the hetrogeneity within class. The relevant literature also points to the greater influence in certain societies of certain properties over others. In some education is the most influential factor in the process of allocation into class positions, while other factors take priority in other societies. The variables used here are labelled as class related ingredients. They are treated with regard to their contribution to the process of allocation to class positions.

Table 4.9. Class Structure by Class Ingredients: 1961, 1972, 1983 (Percentages)

Ingre-dients	Religion Jews	Arabs	Sex Male	Female	Ethnicity Seph.	Others	Age < 30	>30	Education Elemen.	Higher	Immigrated Before 1948	After 1948
Class*/ Year												
1961	100	—	98	2	6	94	51	49	80	20	83	17
1 1972	9	4	98	2	28	72	40	60	50	50	63	37
1983	97	3	92	8	30	70	47	53	31	69	55	45
1961	91	9	81	19	19	81	44	56	92	8	55	45
2 1972	92	8	80	20	31	69	38	62	59	41	44	56
1983	91	9	81	19	43	57	51	49	50	50	45	55
1961	98	2	61	39	11	89	74	26	55	45	63	37
3 1972	98	2	60	40	16	84	61	40	5	95	54	46
1983	94	6	57	43	27	73	67	33	11	89	55	45
1961	98	2	68	32	21	79	63	37	88	12	51	49
4 1972	96	4	55	45	34	66	57	43	34	66	43	57
1983	96	4	46	54	44	56	66	34	25	75	52	48
1961	92	8	81	19	41	59	69	31	98	2	36	64
5 1972	89	11	81	19	52	48	58	42	76	24	32	68
1983	80	20	78	22	52	48	64	36	62	38	37	63

* Class 1 to 5 as in other tables. Entries in cells rounded to whole units.

The presentation in Table 4.9 includes variables that have not yet been discussed. Further explanation of these variables is provided later. For the present purpose, age, level of education, and year of immigration appear to be associated with the present class structure; the working-class, the semiautonomous and managers/

professionals classes include more young individuals than the first two classes. The information for 1983, for example, suggests that a higher proportion of young individuals (under 30) tends to be concentrated in the three lower classes. But the difference is not critical. In 1961 the difference between the young and others was much more impressive, about half of the young belonging to the proletariat vs. a third of the non-young who belonged to this class.

Education is a variable which can tell more about class allocation and class composition than age and perhaps even more than gender or ethnicity. The class composition by education reveals some of the specificity of Israel as a society in transition toward a capitalist system. By 1983 the bourgeoisie and petty-bourgeoisie had become more educated. The managers/professionals class, which in 1961 had been more than half populated by individuals with only elementary schooling was, by 1983, the class with the higher proportion of persons with a higher education (89%), as is to be expected from this class in a modern society. The same was also true of the semiautonomous class which in 1961 included only 21% of higher-educated persons, but which by 1983 had gone up to 75%. The increase in education of the entire population also affected the proletariat;[23] about a third of its membership in 1983 had higher education (note, however, that this includes both high school and university levels) ranging from incomplete high school to university graduate level.

Year of immigration, or *Vetek* (seniority) in the new society is a general specification of an immigrant society. It is assumed and has already been validated in the literature, that year of immigration is an important factor in the process of allocation to class positions, and in reallocation, or mobility, between classes.[24] Some authors suggest that the last wave of immigrants enters the bottom ranks of the economy, and then is "pushed up" by the next wave of immigration.[25] This is, of course, an unwarranted supposition since important assets such as capital or education may transcend the hardship of absorption into the class structure.

This ingredient had a substantive influence in 1961, regarding Classes 1 to 5, that were dominated by veterans. The proletariat class was already in 1961 a class of newcomers. The effect of this factor became less during the period, the proportion of veterans in Class 1 going down from 88% to 55%, from 55% to 45% in Class 2, and from 63% to 55% in Class 3. This process is anticipated because of the natural decrease in the proportion of prestatehood immigrants who still were in the labor force in 1983 (and also the increased proportion in the labor force of Israeli-born), and also because of the decrease in the number of immigrants. This means that the core of recruitment to class positions shifted from immigration as the prime base of labor to the outcomes of the natural growth of the population and to the reservoir in the occupied territories. Inspection of a reverse distribution—years of immigration by class structure—reveals a reduction of veterans in the proletariat (1961 vs. 1983).

A more rigorous analysis is needed in order to specify the direction and intensity of the effects of the above factors on the process of allocation to class positions. This will be dealt with below. Yet it is very possible to indicate the potential odds of individuals with certain properties attaining less-attractive class positions than others. This is attempted in Table 4.10 by specifying the percentages of certain categories in Classes 1 to 5.

Table 4.10. Class Structure Composition: Women, Sephardim, Non-Jews, and Seniority; 1961, 1972, 1983 (Percentages)

Category/Class and year		Women	Seph.	Non-Jews	Seniority
	1961	1.9	6.3	0.0	82.7
1	1972	1.7	27.6	3.6	63.2
	1983	7.8	29.7	3.1	54.8
	1961	19.0	18.9	9.4	55.2
2	1972	19.9	30.7	7.0	44.2
	1983	18.8	43.4	9.0	44.9
	1961	39.4	11.1	2.0	62.5
3	1972	39.9	15.7	2.0	54.1
	1983	42.8	26.7	6.0	54.9
	1961	31.7	21.1	2.0	51.2
4	1972	44.8	33.6	3.6	43.1
	1983	54.3	44.3	5.6	51.7
	1961	18.8	41.2	7.9	36.0
5	1972	18.1	51.8	10.0	32.0
	1983	21.8	52.0	19.8	36.5

The class structure composition in terms of gender, ethnic origin, religion, and years of immigration underwent a process of change which was neither even nor drastic. The capitalist/bourgeoisie class remained predominantly Jewish, male, Ashkenazi, and veteran. The petty-bourgeoisie was changed by the proportion of the Sephardim which attained over 43% of this class membership in the 1980s. Class 4 became dominated in 1983 by women and included many Sephardim. By 1983 the proletariat was mainly Jewish, male, Sephardi and nonveteran, but included non-Jews in a higher proportion than their overall share of the labor market. Females also became overrepresented in this class.

The entries in the next table may indicate the "twisted" association between minority characteristics (gender, ethnicity, and so forth) and class structure distribution. Minorities in Israel as defined in social terms but not necessarily in proportion to their numbers seem to be subjected to the fate of their comparative groups in other capitalist countries. The share of certain minority groups in certain classes, is much more than their share in the labor force.

Table 4.11. Percentage of Women, Non-Jews, Sephardim, and Nonveterans in the Labor Force: 1961, 1972, 1983

Period/Category*	1961	1972	1983
Women	25.4	29.8	36.8
Non-Jews	5.7	6.1	9.8
Sephardim	25.9	34.2	40.3
Nonveterans **	49.8	51.0	52.1

*   Entries based on samples of the above years. This is, in a few cases, different from the information which is based on the entire survey. See Chapter 1.

** Percentage of nonveterans (after 1948) as a share of the entire population including Israeli-born.

The nonmediated observation of the class structure in 1961, 1972 and 1983, suggests that Israeli society is approaching the form of a class structure in a capitalist society in basic shape and parameters. As in capitalist societies the minorities in Israel such as women, Sephardim, and non-Jews are more likely than the majority (the hegemonic group) to occupy the less-attractive positions in the economy. But it should be immediately noted that the categories more vulnerable to placement in the proletariat or the intracapitalist contradictory locations are, except for non-Jews, actually a proportional majority in the entire population or even the labor force in which, the Sephardim, for example, increased their share to almost 40%. However, the sheer number of women, Sephardim and non-Jews is not the main reason for their weakness in the labor market, or more precisely, in the process of production. Their relative lack of either capital or other resources such as education makes them a minority in terms of allocation into class positions and correlatively of the rewards that are derived by being in this location.

To sum up at this stage, these groups are more divorced from ownership of means of production and authority than others. Thus, they are more subject to the authority of others and to the fluctuations of the labor market than the majority groups. In other words, being a proletarian means what it is has always meant regarding material and nonmaterial rewards and selling of labor in the market. Being a woman and/or Sephardi or non-Jew indicates a greater likelihood of being proletarian or also of being located in Class 5 than for other groups. This needs to be more thoroughly examined in order to suggest more substantive conclusions regarding the class structure, the process of class positions allocation and to a certain extent of class boundaries.

NOTES

1. Handlin, 1973.
2. Segev, 1984; Sicron, 1957; Lissak, Mizrachi et al., 1969; Bernstein, 1981.
3. Sicron, 1957; Klinov-Malul, 1986.
4. A position of management in the Histadrut economy is indeed different from that of management in the private sector. See Ben-Porat, 1979. While building a class structure, information on class-cum-sector (of individual's positions) was not pursued here. Thus management is aggregated here without any internal specification such as the sector.
5. The managers' position in the capitalist system is defined in various terms in the literature. Some see them as fulfilling a function of exploiting others for the benefit of the capitalist system, see Poulantzas, 1975. See also, Wright, 1978, 1985; Carchedi, 1977; Ehrenreich and Ehrenreich, 1971, on the debate on the managers' position in class structure.
6. See Note 16, Chapter 3.
7. See, for example, Lewin-Epstein and Semyonov, 1986; Rosenfeld, 1962; Rustum, 1973; Carmi and Rosenfeld, 1974; Zureik, 1976. More information, not yet systematically presented, can be derived from various statistics on labor conditions in the Arab sector, Israeli (Ben-Porath, 1966) and non-Israeli citizens, and in the daily and weekly newspapers.
8. Wright and Singleman, 1982.
9. Singlemann, 1978.
10. Goran, 1981.
11. Ben-Porath, 1986; CBS various years.
12. For the ongoing debate on class and gender, see Goldthorpe, 1983; Crompton and Man, 1986; Britten and Heat, 1983; Heat and Britten 1984; West, 1982; Erikson, 1984; Hartmann, 1976, 1981. As mentioned in the text, this study does not elaborate on class-cum-gender in greater depth than the presentation of class structure by gender. While the class structure of women in Israel may be as presented here, it is incomplete.
13. Ben-Porath, 1986.
14. Amir, 1986.
15. Wright, 1982; Goran, 1981.
16. Ben-Porat, 1987a; also Bodnar, 1977; Rosenblum, 1973; Piory, 1979.
17. Sicron, 1957.
18. Ben-Porath, 1986. It should be noted here that the percentage of Israeli-born in 1983 is biased.

19. Ben-Porath, 1986. This is first of all dependent on a political solution which might put an end to the Israeli occupation of the West Bank (Judea and Samaria) and the Gaza strip.
20. Ben-Porath, 1966; Rosenfeld, 1962.
21. Ben-Porath, 1966, 1986.
22. Research is indeed proliferating and some of the major works are cited later. They are mostly related to the study of mobility, and/or the allocation of individuals to roles/occupations and statuses.
23. Amir, 1986.
24. Hartman, 1981.
25. Lewin-Epstein and Semyonov, 1986. See also Ben-Porath, 1986; Eisenstadt, 1985, Liberson, 1970.

5

Becoming a Class Member:
The Process of Allocation

The previous chapter paints a general portrait of the fivefold class structure in Israel at three points of time, each of which is supposed to reflect the class structure of a certain decade within the overall studied period. This chapter deals with the same class structure and the same parameters, but is devoted to the presentation of some aspects of the process of allocation to class structure positions. This is a major process involved in the more fundamental process of class structure formation. The process of class allocation (in Israel) has been responsible for the absorption of immigrants into positions in the economy and, correlatively, to other "statuses" in general society. It has been responsible for the recruitment of domestic labor power to the class structure as well as the reshaping of class boundaries, although to a lesser degree than the process of creation of class structure positions. The process of allocation to class positions is treated by sociological literature under a different name and more importantly, using different assumptions than that of class. This is evident in the research on mobility or "status attainment",[1] with very few students considering class as a unit of social stratification rather than occupation.[2]

The study of allocation to class or status, or just occupational positions in the social structure (the definition of the studied unit is, as already noted, a matter of theory), centers on definite factors that are assumed to provide most of the necessary explicanda by use of a regression-type model. In this model the net effect of certain factors on the process of class position or status, or other allocation is estimated. The literature specifies education, work experience, ethnic origin, socioeconomic background, and some other factors as the explanatory bundle of variables, each of which has both an autonomous influence and some influence through its association with other variables. In short, it is suggested by the literature that one's individual position in society—referring mainly to status in the labor market—is determined in part by merit, and in part by inheritance from one's immediate background. This is valid both for the stage of entering the labor market and for the opportunities of mobility.

It should be noted that the real story of becoming assigned to class position is only one chapter in a continual process of class formation. The detailed quantative analysis of the effects of various factors on the odds of the individual being assigned to the capitalist, managerial, proletarian or other classes cannot exactly or reliably reflect the basic social processes that either set up the opportunities for some people to attain qualifications, or maintain premarket social associations enabling certain people to be qualified for better (or worse) class positions. However, the quantative analysis of effects of selected factors can inform us about their relative importance in allocating individuals to class positions and whether this has changed during the period after 1948.

This study's ultimate interest is with the form and content of class structure in Israel rather than with a detailed discussion of the process of class structure formation in terms of formative agents and social conflict. Thus the following extensive estimation of the contribution of certain factors is in line with this study's prime concern; some of the factors included in the explicandum may also be considered as autonomous potential components of the processes of group identification and of formation of an alternative social antagonism around a different cleavage than that of class relations. The history of Israeli society after statehood includes an experience of ethnic antagonism and explicit attempts to build up ethnic-based identification. The predominant process of state building exemplfies what some may consider to be an integrating process, overriding other processes of partial identification, or even as a process which actually suppresses class formation.

In this study the process of allocation to class positions is approximated by the use of six variables available for this purpose. Three out of the six, gender, ethnic origin and religion, have been proved to cause conflicts, breaks, and social reorganization.[3] Thus they can be considered as potential bases of identifications other than class, or as associating or competing with the process of class formation. The major conflict that has engulfed the entire Israeli society including the Israeli Arabs, is the religio-nationalistic conflict that, after 1967 (the Six Days War), breached the boundaries of the society. The point here is the possible competing processes of class and religion (nationality) within the Israeli citizenry. Hence the lot of the Israeli Arabs may be explained by their being a minority pressurized by a political situation in which citizenship, religion, and nationality contradict each other to a degree sufficient to prevent the consolidation of class structure by class ingredients alone.

To turn to a gender-based conflict in Israel, the organization of women on a competing political level is very sparse. The assumed position of women in the prestate, so-called "pioneering" society, has been proven a legend more than a reality.[4] In practice only very few shared the same power as men in the economy and in politics. The mass immigration of many Jews from semifeudal societies just made matters worse. The low percentage of women in the labor force in the early 1950s and then their increasing distribution in class positions of property and power is an indication of their potential. The previous presentation of the distribution of women in class structure positions reaffirmed a certain and consistent correlation between gender and class in Israel. Also it is worth remembering this gender's tendency to be concentrated in contradictory locations. It is suggested here that the immediate and quantitative differences between basic class positions and contradictory class positions in Israel is less important than the effects of the latter on class structure formation and correlatively, on social transformation. The class-cum-gender distribution may affect the transformation of the class structure in opposite ways. That is, it may either enhance or hinder the transformation of the class structure and of society as a whole.

The variables used here to enlarge on the process of allocation of individuals to class positions are as follows, starting with the dependent variable and then with the independent ones:

Class-structure: This is the fivefold class scheme that has been presented before. It is arranged in hierarchical order: bourgeoisie, petty-bourgeoisie, managers/ professionals, semiautonomous, and proletariat. The reasons for hierarchy are first of all theoretical and can be traced in a few ascending steps; the classes reflect the division between property owners and others. Thus the prime class dividing line is between bourgeoisie, petty-bourgeoisie, and the rest of the classes. Then the division by control over labor processes redraws the lines and moves the managers up (but may push the petty-bourgeoisie out, since they are in positions of property but not of control over labor).

By the criteria that Wright uses the hierarchical order within the classes of the capitalist mode of production is explicit. However, this is not so when other classes in the scheme are also included. According to the basic argument of the origin of class, the petty-bourgeoisie belong to a different mode of production, and although this class shares the same social formation with the capitalist class or the proletariat, the relationships between them are not those of a gradual/quantitative order. The division is between two historically different modes. Any attempt to treat them on the same level, although possible to certain extent, needs to be justified.

In the following this is taken into consideration. Of the six possible classes in the present scheme, that of kibbutz/cooperative was dropped. It seems improper to treat this class on the same level as the first five classes precisely because of the above-mentioned reason. The ensuing analysis of the class scheme in Israel is arranged in stages. It starts with presentation of all classes (without regard to the origin of their mode of production), and then discusses a shorter version of the class scheme that combines some classes into one category, assuming them to be sufficiently close in several substantive class ingredients.

Gender: The internal composition of a gender category in Israel should be noted, particularly because this has a determinative effect on the tendency of women to participate in the labor market and thus to enter the class structure without the

mediation of spouse or family. Important characteristics which influence participation in the labor force are, first, ethnic composition—women originating in Asia or
Africa tend to participate less in the labor market. Second, age and marriage have
an effect on the tendency to work outside the home. Third, education makes a
considerable difference, while fourth, religion has an enclaving effect. Women from
the most orthodox sectors tend to participate less in the labor market, and if they
do, they are confined to "regional economies," that is, near home, within the
religious community and in such positions as teachers, shopkeepers, and in computer-
related work.[5]

Some of these intervening characteristics relating to a gender-cum-class correlation are taken care of in this study by other presented variables.

Age: The age groups specified here start at 21, the age where this study's sample
began to select the candidates for further analysis, and continue to the age of 65, the
official retirement age for males in Israel. These limits were chosen because the
ultimate aim of this study is to examine class structure through the positions in the
process of production, not through mere counting of individuals. The age of 65 is the
upper limit, yet because the official retirement age of women is 62, the principle of
dealing only with active labor force is partly impaired, as it is by the possiblity
that capitalists and self-employed do not retire, so their estimated rate in the class
structure is affected by using age as a limit of sample selection. This factor is
assumed to have only a negligible effect.

Three age groups are arranged in order to satisfy the particular needs of this
analysis: twenty-one to thirty, thirty-one to forty, and forty-one to sixty-five. (Too
many groups are a burden on a long-linear regression analysis.) The first group
includes individuals after their military service entering their first stages in the
economy. Some students suggest that this is the most unstable period in individual
careers; a person may move between jobs—not neccessarily in an upward direction—
until settling down, building a family and starting a life-time career.[6] This is also a
stage when many young people are engaged in attaining higher education. These
individuals have passed the age-selection criteria for this study and they are
included in the samples. However, since they could not provide evidence that they
were located in a class position (through the information on occupation and participation in the labor force gathered by the CBS), students who were not in the labor
force are excluded.

The second age group includes individuals who are either in their first stage of
building a career after already setting up a family or being close to the top rungs of
their career, but have some way yet to go. It can be assumed that these individuals
have already experienced some mobility, and as they approach the upper limit of
this group (forty years old), their career path is almost mapped out. The likelihood
that they will experience dramatic mobility in either class or status is thus
diminished.

The third group, ages forty-one to sixty-five, is quite heterogeneous. It is
improper to treat an individual in his forties like someone in his sixties and close to

retirement. This group includes individuals who are struggling to reach the top of their profession, individuals who have already given up hope of moving up, and those who are preparing their after-work career. However, it is maintained here that in class terms the age groups in this aggregation have something in common— the class assignment in structural terms is almost final. The sons of the bourgeoisie are now inheriting their family property, those of farming stock have already joined the family farm and so on. The individuals in management will remain in this class and so will those in semiautonomus positions, with some possibility of moving up to management. As for the proletariat, their lot is already assigned. The probabilities of moving up are almost nil.

In accordance with the theme of this study, age is treated here as a factor related to the process of allocation of individuals to class positions. Thus the effect of age on recruitment to class or on mobility between classes is sought here.

Education: This variable needs very little explanation. Any study on allocation of individuals into class positions (or statuses as some authors prefer) treats this variable as a key contributor, for instance, as a sum of years of education that one accumulates through formal schooling or as distinct levels of education, such as elementary, high school, or university level, which are considered as having qualitative differences. Whatever the measure one uses, it is apparent that education makes a real contribution to one's odds of joining a class position.

The development and expansion of education in Israel was reported in brief in the second chapter of this study. As shown, the amount of education increased, as indicated by the average of years of schooling in the 1950s, 1970s, and 1980s and by the proportion of individuals with higher education (over thirteeen years) in the labor force in these periods. Nonetheless, the raising of the level of education over the forty years did not bring about a dramatic change in the ethnic gap. All groups of ethnic origin gained more formal education and all improved their position in the absolute educational gain over the years. Hence the most disadvantaged categories climbed the educational ladder, but so did the less disadvantaged. Eventually all categories remained at almost the same distance from each other, although on higher rungs than before.[7] As evidence shows, the overall gap between Asian/African Jews and European/American Jews thus remained about the same from 1961 to 1982.

This information is a preview to the following analysis: the anticipated effect of education as allocating mechanism is practically interrelated to that of ethnicity, gender, and religion, that is, there is a structural correlation between these variables. But it is likely that each may have a *sui generic* contribution to the process of allocation to class positions. A priori it seems that education and this process share common variance, the size of which still needs to be decided.

Education is divided here into three divisions: none-at-all or only elementary school together constitute one division. High school (nine to twelve years) constitutes the second division, and the third division includes thirteen years and over, university (incomplete and complete) and certain other institutions of higher education.

Ethnic Origin: The number of countries of origin of Jews in Israel in the 1980s amounts to more than 100, but there was substantial emigration from only a few of them. The CBS arranges the countries of origin into the following general categories: Asia (middle-eastern, far-eastern countries and so forth), Africa (Morocco, Egypt, South Africa), Europe (U.S.S.R. Poland, Germany, Finland, United Kingdom, Portugal and so on), and America (Canada, the United States, Central and South America). These are rearranged here into three categories: born in Israel, Asia/Africa, and Europe/America. The drawbacks of this division (and that of the CBS) are acknowledged; individuals from countries of very low socioeconomic levels at the time of emigration are combined with individuals from a very high level of development, as in the Europe/America category.[8] This means that the variance within an ethnic category may be more than between any of the three major ethnic categories. If one wishes to explicate the effect of country of emigration on one's odds of being allocated to a class position in Israel, the above division into categories is not the most effective one. Yet this division still dominates the formal coding of statistical information in Israel, and it should be noted that it is quite productive in several respects. In characteristics such as education the difference between Sephardim (Asian/African Jews) and Ashkenazim (European/American Jews) reflected a real situation, and hence was informative.

The percentage of Sephardim in the 1948 population was low, increased during the period and reached 50% in the 1980s. This figure includes Israelis born to parents from this category. It seems that although the correlation has relaxed over the years, an ethnic origin-cum-class exists even in the 1980s.

The country-of-origin variable is used here following the conventional division by the CBS; Asia/Africa, Europe/America and Israeli-born.

Year of Immigration: More than one study, whether in economics, sociology or both, when carried out in immigration countries (Canada, Australia, Israel or the United States) specifies the importance of immigration period in the general pattern of immigrant absorption and, in particular, the redistribution of immigrants to the class structure.[9] It is suggested, for instance, that as a result of newcomers entering the lower ranks of industry and services as proletariat, the positions of veterans may improve, moving up within the same class, closer to its borderline, and becoming supervisors, foremen and so forth. However year of immigration is associated with imported assets. Newcomers with higher education or with capital may be repositioned in nonproletarian class locations. Alternatively, class position in the country of emigration may still be effective to some degree in the process of allocation of individual immigrants in the class structure of the country of destination.

The mass immigration from 1948 to 1952 reshaped the class structure. With the influx of capital more individuals occupied positions in industry, building and services, and fewer in agriculture. The veteran Jews who immigrated before 1948 improved their inter- or intra-class positions—they became managers in industry and building, administrators in goverment or local services, police and army. The immigrants of the 1960s were better equiped educationally than their predecessors and thus they were able to enter the middle of the class structure more often than their predecessors.[10] In fact, during the period the effect of year of immigration began to fade. For the immigrants of the 1970s and 1980s, the quality of human resources, the policy of the government, and the decrease in the number of immigrants enabled them to enter different (and better) class positions, and probably, for a smaller proportion of them to become proletariat.

The year of immigration variable is divided here into four groups: the first includes those who were in Israel before 1948. The other three groups include immigrants from 1948 to 1964, from 1965 to 1970, and after 1971. These categories are suggested by CBS in the censuses of 1972 and 1983. For the sample of 1961, this year was the last group. Later on this variable was divided into before and after immigration.

Religion/Culture: Israel's population in 1983 included about 17% of non-Jews, about 80% of whom were Moslems and almost all the rest, Christians, Arabs, and Druse. The number as well as the proportion of non-Jews increased from 1948 to the 1980s.[11] Their participation in the labor force also increased. This category constituted an instructive example of a minority. They were citizens who cast their votes in elections to the political institutions of the state, they could associate with Israeli political parties as members or sympathizers, but in the 1950s they were confined to certain regions and were subjected to military government. Hence they could not participate in the labor market where they could have gained some advantages over certain groups of newcomers. In the 1960s the Arab population in Israel began to enter the country's economy in full force. However, Arabs were not admitted to certain government jobs, and many Israeli employers refrained from positioning Arabs in authority locations with powers of supervision over Jewish employees. Hence the "Arab economy" was divided, being either in the least preferred positions in the general economy or remaining within the Arab religious enclave.

The entrance of Arabs from the occupied territories had some effect on the position of Israeli Arabs. However, considering the labor market or the economy in general, the change was not overly critical. In the main, the Israeli Arabs in the labor force remained as they were, with some changes regarding the Arab economy or their distribution in the Israeli economy. As indicated by the information in Chapter 4, the Israeli Arabs deepened their hold on the proletariat.

The religious variable is divided here into two groups—Jews and Arabs. The latter constitute the non-Jewish category that also includes Christian Arabs, Druze and others.

There follow the seven variables that are now subjected to analysis in order to estimate the effects of six of them on the seventh—the class position in the class structure. The process of allocation to class position is not initiated by these variables, but they affect the process by their influence on selecting or screening the distribution of "proper" individuals to positions in the economy. The point is that positions in the class structure are the effects of structural factors; those responsible for the class structure (and its creation) set the degrees of freedom or limits to the process of allocations. The basic contention of this study is that the process of creation of class structure positions predominates in the process of allocation of individuals to these positions. However, the odds of the individual being assigned to a class (not by subjective intention, but by subjective selection between given sets of alternatives) depend upon his assets/capacities. Nonetheless, in a class structure where the demand for semiautonomous positions is limited, education may be a less effective asset, and individuals with higher education may have to occupy less attractive (probably proletarian or close to proletarian) positions, or to emigrate. A regression model could not explain this, but the same model repeated at different times (or one that incorporates time as a variable) can be of much value.

Estimation of the effect of the above variables on class position is executed here by a log-linear procedure. This is the procedure that treats a model that includes categorical variables and is considered as an effective procedure for this purpose.[12] The present model includes both categorical and continuous variables. The dependent variable in this study is hierarchical, but has no special merit in the present procedure. The ultimate aim is to estimate the same parameters in each period separately. Table 5.1 treats the main effects of class and a portion of the interaction terms—that portion established between the dependent variable (class) and each of the six independent variables presented above.

Table 5.1 presents the parameters for each period. As will be seen, the interpretation of these parameters is less than straightforward.

As a first step in a partial analysis of the association between gender, age, ethnic origin, religion, education and year of immigration, with class position, the information in Table 5.1 is not particularly unequivocal; by the measures of association and by the goodness-of-fit statistics, the results leave much to be desired in terms of model fitting. However, the prime interest here is with the effects of the above factors on the class allocation process over the three consequential periods. There is a suspicion that some of the weakness of the results of the model are connected with the way this particular model was executed. The basic model is the multiple combination of seven variables, (class and six other variables, with different values in each), producing a $5 \cdot 2 \cdot 3 \cdot 3 \cdot 2 \cdot 3 \cdot 2 = 1080$ cell contingency dimension.

This probably causes many cells to be empty in the complete contingency matrix.[14] The relatively poor model fit here is an outcome of the concrete model-fitting parameters estimation.

A surface review of the parameters in Table 5.1—every single variable's interaction with class vs. a reference variable—indicates the inconclusive state of the class variables of 1961; the variance is too wide to allow a definite parameter to be statistically stable. The state of the classes in 1972 and 1983 is much more stable than in 1961. Gender seems to have no effect in 1961, but did have an effect in 1972 and 1983. Age had a greater effect in 1961 than in future periods. Country of origin

Table 5.1. Parameters Estimation: Gender, Age, Ethnic Origin, Religion, Education, Year of Immigration, and Class; 1961, 1972, 1983

Variables/Year	1961	1972	1983
Class			
1	-16.738	-3.210*	2.140*
2	4.412	.825*	.054
3	3.889	-.149	- .227*
4	3.821	1.053*	1.187*
Class/Gender			
1	7.582	1.197*	.478*
2	-1.704	-.100	.270*
3	-2.145	-.427*	-.095
4	-2.050	.604*	.638*
Class/Age			
1	-.005	-.128	-.337*
2	-.383*	-.201*	-.069
3	.342*	.106*	.044
4	.010	.085	.045
Class/Ethnic Origin			
1	-.501	.010	-.436*
2	.109	.015	.100
3	-.184	-.327*	-.066
4	.124	.024	.078
Class/Religion			
1	7.084	.422*	.448
2	-2.256	-.090	-.128
3	-1.353	.033	.099
4	-1.280	-.076	.147
Class/Education			
1	-.234	.168	-.105
2	.210*	.341*	.270*
3	.861*	-1.181*	.671*
4	.001	-.060	-.119
Class/Year of Immigration			
1	.554*	.514	.005
2	-.148*	-.229*	.003
3	-.003	.219	.070
4	-.059	.003	.050
Entropy**	.132	.162	.117
Concentration	.123	.144	.118
Likelihood ratio			
Chi Square	141.026	213.991	182.295
P	.057	.000	.000

* Z-value equal or greater than 2.

** Entropy and concentration measure the strength of association between the dependent and the predictor variables.[13]

affected certain class positions. Religion would seem to have been ineffective in this model combination, but as is explained later, it was actually the factor of discrimination that marked a line between the two religious groups. To be Jewish or not made a considerable difference in class position terms. As anticipated, education had a concrete influence on some of the class positions, but year of immigration seems to have been an inconclusive factor.

A partial solution to these indeterminate results is suggested in the next two tables. Table 5.2 is a replication of Table 5.1, but the class scheme is rearranged into three classes only; Class 1 now includes bourgeoisie and petty-bourgeoisie; Class 2 includes managers and the semiautonomous, and Class 3 is, as before, the proletariat. The independent variables have been dichotomized. This reduces the contingency table into 3·2·2·2·2·2·2=192 cells, a still-complex cell-dimension contingencies table, but more open to interpretation.

Table 5.2 estimates parameters for the main effects of a threefold class scheme, and the interaction of six independent variables with this class scheme. Each was dichotomized before being subjected to analysis. The dichotomized variables are as follows:

Gender—remains unchanged. Age—divided into young (up to forty years old) and old (over forty). Education—divided into none + elementary, and higher (nine years or more). Religion—divided into Jews and non-Jews. Ethnic origin—divided into Sephardim and others (Ashkenazim and Israeli-born). Year of immigration—immigrants who came to Israel before 1948 and those thereafter.

Table 5.3 deals only with the main effects of the variables (no interactions) regarding the 5·2·3·3·2·3·2 contingencies table. Main effects of class and six variables are estimated.

Inspection of Table 5.3 and the previous table allows a summing review of the influence of the six variables upon allocation to class position.

Gender interaction with class was effective in 1961, remaining so in 1972 and in 1983. It seems that in 1983 the main effect of gender was less than in 1972, but the gender-class effect was still there in 1983.

A technical clarification would be useful here. The log-linear procedure produces estimations of the required parameters by eliminating the first groups in each category; this constitutes the reference group for estimating the net effect of other group(s). Thus in Table 5.3 class parameters are those of Classes 2 and 3 compared to Class 1, which is used as a comparative reference group in the present case. Thus, for example, it appears that being a woman adds "more fraction of a point" on class location. Table 5.2 made it possible to estimate gender and interaction with different classes and also interaction of the latter with other variables. Age was also affective, mainly in association with Class 2. Country of origin had a relatively small but significant effect. Religion had a significant effect. Education produced a negative effect with regard to Class 3—the proletariat (as expected), and year of immigration had a waning effect approaching 1983.

Table 5.2. Parameters Estimation: Gender, Age, Ethnic Origin, Religion, Education,
Year of Immigration, and Three Categories of Class; 1961, 1972, 1983*

Year/Variable	1961	1972	1983
Class			
1	-.151	-.401*	-.773*
2	.112	.168	.530*
Gender			
1	.158*	.168*	.366*
2	.285*	-.326*	-.431*
Age			
1	-.315*	-.213*	-.184*
2	.182*	.055	-.006
Origin			
1	-.099*	-.048	-.098*
2	-.166*	-.162*	-.091*
Religion			
1	-.280*	-.003	.096
2	.583*	.243*	.298*
Education			
1	-.036	.108	.026
2	-.648*	-.613*	-.448*
Year of Immigration			
1	.059	.076	.028
2	.121*	.091*	.078
Entropy	.130	.176	.133
Concentration	.147	.207	.159
Likelihood			
Chi Square	96.742	146.622	124.431
P	.001	.000	.000

* Z-value equal to or greater than 2

The parameters that are estimated by the log-linear procedure can be used as
regression-like coefficients, and these can be used to obtain log-odds coefficients

that lend themselves to easier interpretation.[15] This is done by multiplying the parameters by 2, and then using the anti-log to convert the model's log-odds into odds.
This is carried out and presented in the following, for the main effects of the six
independent variables.

Table 5.3. Parameters Estimation: Main Effects of Gender, Age, Ethnic Origin,
Religion, Education, and Year of Immigration: 1961, 1972, 1983

Year/Variable	1961	1972	1983
Class			
1	-9.375	-2.937*	-1.906*
2	2.056	.751*	-.212*
3	2.522	.030	.753*
4	2.271*	.989*	.776*
Gender			
1	2.271	.716*	.185*
Age			
1	-.227*	-.309*	-.047
2	.025	-.177*	-.111*
Origin			
1	-.466*	.159*	.675*
2	.596*	.745*	.724*
Religion			
1	1.252*	1.435*	1.084*
Education			
1	.408*	.235*	-.257*
2	.420*	.314*	.267*
Year of Immigration			
1	.156*	-.078*	-.023

* Z-value equal to or greater than 2

Each entry in Table 5.4 indicates the main effect of the particular ingredient in
terms of odds. For instance, the effect of being a woman on assigment to class was
insignificant in 1961, but was highly significant by 1972.

The model outcomes can now be partly evaluated in terms of odds that refer,
however, to the main effects alone. At present these indicate the extent of the
changes during the period. It appears that minority characteristics had a significant influence; religion, ethnic origin and gender (for the less advantaged category
in each) made a difference. This bears out the indications in the previous chapter
that women, Arabs, and Sephardim are overrepresented in middle or lower classes.

Table 5.4. Odds of Gender, Age, Ethnic Origin, Religion, Education, and Year of Immigration: 1961, 1972, 1983

Period/Variable*		1961	1972	1983
Gender	1	—	27.039	2.344
Age	1	.351	.240	—
	2	—	.442	.599
Ethnic Origin	1	.116	2.079	22.387
	2	15.559	30.902	28.05
Religion	1	319.153	714.310	147.231
Education	1	6.546	2.951	.306
	2	6.918	4.246	3.419
Year of Immigration	1	2.051	.698	—

* Variables as in Table 5.3.

Hence the factors assumed to be related to the process of allocation of individuals to class positions seem to fulfill their function as suggested. It should be recalled that the explication here is from a structural and causal perspective. Thus it is proposed that the process of allocation of individuals into class position is preceded (though not in exactly geometrical terms), or at least conditioned, by the process of creation of class positions. The association between these processes is determined by sociohistorical factors at the level of the entire social structure, some of which have been earlier noted. It is impossible to elaborate on the association between class creating and class allocating processes through the regression-like procedure utilized here to explicate the latter process. The particular conclusions about these two processes in Israel since 1948 will be discussed in Chapter 8. This chapter testifies to the (estimated) effects of gender, religion and ethnic origin in particular. These factors go beyond what others consider to be ingredients of attainment of social position (status, class, and so forth); they are potential bases of group/category formation, which may compete with class structure formation and, in certain conditions, demote class formation, replacing it with other group formations that center on nonclass cleavage. The Israeli scene at the end of the 1960s and the start of the 1970s, for example, was dominated by ethnic protests and by some attempt at consolidation of ethnic group formation. The effect of the religious factor needs no elaboration here, as it is openly evident in Israeli society.

NOTES

1. Lipset and Zetterberg, 1959; Goldthorpe, 1980; Duncan, 1966; Hauser et al., 1975; Hazelring and Garnier, 1976; Hauser and Featherman, 1977; Stewart et al., 1980.
2. Goldthorpe, 1980; Erikson et al., 1982; Robinson, 1984; Wright, 1982.
3. In more than one historical case, ethnicity and religion coincided and accelerated social conflict. Gender, in comparison to the first two, seems to have been the least enhancing cause for general conflict in society. See Crompton and Mann, 1986.
4. Bernstein, 1981.
5. Ben-Porath, 1986; Shelhev and Friedman, 1985.
6. Miller and Form, 1980.
7. Hartman, 1981; Ben-Porath, 1986; Hercowitz, 1976.
8. Taylor and Hudson, 1972.
9. Evans and Kelley, 1984; Hartman, 1981.
10. Sicron, 1957.
11. Ben-Porath, 1986.
12. Aldrich and Forrest, 1984; Knoke and Burk, 1980.
13. Haberman, 1982.
14. It is possible to utilize a correction technique to deal with the problem of empty cells in the matrix. However, this has little effect on the basic problem of lack of information. See SPSSX, 1986.
15. SPSSX, 1986; also, Knoke and Burk, 1980.

6

Reallocation:
Up and Down in the Class Structure

There is some truth in the assertion that a modern society is characterized by mobility. This was partly true in nonmodern societies also, however the proponents of this assertion have made their point quite unequivocally; in modern, essentially capitalist, societies, mobility is open, thus the ones who are equipped with the qualifications required by society, mainly by the economic market are likely to be mobile, that is, to gain a better class position or to mantain a good one. This is also true in a reverse process; those whose qualifications are obsolete are likely to be down graded.

There is little study of class mobility. Research on mobility tends to take occupation, status and related variables as its major interest.[1] This research is undertaken in accordance with the modernization, or growth, perspective; mobility is conceptualized as a product of an open, competitive and merit-based society, in which individuals become mobile through their own capability and efforts. Most importantly, it is the structure of society that is considered responsible for the options of mobility. That is, the particular structure of a capitalist society makes it possible for the more talented to gain better positions, mainly in terms of socioeconomic status .[2]

Following this line of thought, some studies although appearing to lend support to the above perspective are also highly critical of many of its core propositions. The thesis that the mobility patterns of industrial societies are similar is countered, partly rejected, and replaced, by other propositions.[3] According to Erikson and his associates industrial societies have a fairly distinctive "mobility profile."[4] They are distinguished because of the differences in their histories that have affected their class structure formation. Yet there are a few common features in the process of class structure formation in capitalist societies, or those that are approaching this formation, including a rapid reduction in the agricultural sector and a rise in industry and services. Thus capitalist societies should have more than a few common characteristics of social mobility because of the mere fact that they are dominated by the capitalist mode of production. However, internal composition such as that involving ethnicity and religion, or different avenues of economic growth such as immigration, have a concrete and sometimes critical effect on internal processes. The mobility process is just one highly indicative example of the significant differences between these societies.

The evolving research on social mobility has been able to formulate its particular concepts. Structural mobility and exchange or circular mobility are noted here because this division is efficient relevant to the present analysis of mobility in Israel as part of the process of allocation to class positions.[5]

Structural changes in the social system constitute the raison d'être of mobility between occupations, jobs and classes. Thus the greater the changes in the social structure, the more substantive is their effect on mobility. A change in the mode of production (such as the transition toward a capitalist system) is accompanied by creation of new positions in the economy and in an enforced process of reallocation as well as fresh recruitment to the new order of positions. Here the major interest is with the structural changes and their effect on class structure or on the combination of intraclass positions. In real society there is an implied association between the creation of positions and their being occupied; they are causally related processes. The change in the structure of class positions makes mobility possible, yet the particular processes and factors that enhance or deter one's mobility are relatively independent of the process of creation of positions. This is due to the conditions in each specific society that affect the odds of moving up or down. The relatively new line of research into capitalist societies concerning the effects of split or dual markets points to (the possible) ethnic/cultural factors that intentionally interfere in a capitalist market, divide the market into two different layers, and affect the odds of social mobility.[6]

Structural mobility is defined in the literature as the mobility that is forced on the members of society. Structural mobility is "that part of total observed mobility which is directly attributable to changes in the structure of objective mobility opportunities."[7] As noted earlier, this is distinct from "exhange mobility," that is unassociated with such changes."[8] Besides using the latter in order to determine the proportion of pure mobility while dissecting mobility tables, it may also be useful in probing the factors that determine allocation and reallocation of individuals to class positions. As some suggest, this allows classification of structural changes in order to estimate the degree of openness or social fluidity in a society.[9] First, according to modernization studies, how much is mobility really determined by merit or effort, and second, according to the line followed here, how much of the latter is attained within the limits of the various structural effects?

Explanation of the difference between structural and exchange mobility demands much more than explaining the proportion of instances of mobility that can be attributed to each. As some rightly emphasize, structural mobility is not merely a nuisance factor.[10]. What is suggested here is that instead of occupational mobility being disregarded because it is associated with status and prestige, it should be incorporated in a more inclusive explanation. Occupational mobility results from structural changes and may occur within a class or between classes. So does mobility between work places or even in the same organization. The point at issue is how much of this mobility is involved with the basic factors of a class position definition such as changes in property relations, or of authority relations?

What, then, are the affects and the intensity of the change in the structure, whether enforced by the external factors such as immigration, the international market, or initiated by the structure's institutions (state interference in the market, in redistribution of education and so on). Certain changes in the economy, for example, induce a class structure change; some individuals without investing any personal effort may find that their class position has been transformed. They may find that their particular relations to the labor process have been modified, or that institutional arrangements of society as a whole have been changed following a dramatic shift in one instance of this society. Immigration is a dramatic causal factor regarding class location, though only one of many.

The major effects of structure on mobility in potential and actual situations has been discerned in studies of societies, such as some eastern countries, that have undergone a critical sociohistorical change. In these cases structural changes were intentionally initiated to reshape the class structure. One author specifies two aspects of social transformation that affected mobility in such cases: the distribution of social classes and the distribution of sociooccupational strata that are differentiated on the basis of education, authority, and sector. Taken together these changes may be referred to as a process of state-socialist structural transformation— a sequence of shifts in social structure and mobility accompanying the combined processes of socialization and industrial development.[11] Besides the theoretically related relevancy of the latter the class structure formations in state-socialist countries seem to be similar to those in Israel particularly in regard to the intensity of state intervention.

Structural changes are therefore directly or indirectly responsible for class and occupational mobility in a society. It seems that exchange mobility is far less important than structural mobility, sometimes appearing to be redundant. Exchange mobility is attributed to the potential and actual opportunities afforded, for example, by education but these often are initiated and implemented by the state or its institutions.[12] Thus in order to explicate the process of allocation between classes (upward or downward mobility) it is worth describing the structural constraints that set up limits to mobility.[13]

Since mobility in class terms refers to the changes of positions in the process of production this mobility implies changes in property relations, in authority over people, or over processes of capital investment or labor. Hence when a semi-autonomous employee becomes a manager he changes not merely his occupation or status—both concrete changes—but also his relations with regard to authority over labor processes and even his relations to capital investment if he has become involved in this level of decision-making.[14] Upper-level managers may receive stocks/shares of the capital invested in the enterprise as part of their income. Mobility of class position is always more critical than that of occupation or work-place. There is no necessarily stringent correlation between the two; it is possible to change occupation but not class and vice-versa; however the latter involves more relational changes with one's environment than the former. An engineer who becomes a plant manager remains an engineer by profession but his class position is different, sometimes substantively. In terms of the relatively complex class structure of capitalist society that is used here this may be undramatic—a move from one contradictory class location to another.

Mobility in class terms should be considered in accordance with the major per-spective of this study. Hence factors other than class may be involved in mobility caused primarily by structural changes. Immigration of different ethnic groups who are also differentiated by socioeconomic background may affect mobility by introducing the ethnic component if positions in a certain class are more open to those of a definite ethnic origin than to others. Even the possibility of becoming a capitalist may be affected by cultural divisions.[15.] This accounts for the under- or over-representation of certain individuals in these positions. In brief, even in a capitalist society nonclass elements enter into the process of reallocation and hence affect the opportunities for social mobility.

The literature is generous in specifing the anticipated outcomes of structural changes regarding class structure and mobility. There is near consensus that indus-trialization is accompanied by a reduction in agriculture, increase of the working class, increase in managers and experts, increase of the service class or, following the concepts used here, increase of basic classes and of contradictory class locations. Modern capitalist/industrial society is characterized by a small agricultural frac-tion of class, by proletariat, and service classes (personal and state bureaucracy). As for mobility, cross-national comparison and studies of tables of intergenerational mobility and of status attainment have something in common;[16] they center on the assertion by Hauser and his colleagues that

> apart from differences between societies in occupational structure, all societies share a common, context-invariant occupational mobility regime. Thus it is also expected that in industrial societies occupational mobility is, *cetaris paribus*, confined to near-close occupational groups. This implies that intergeneration mobility tables will be characterized by the predominancy of the diagonal—most of second generation individuals ended up in their parents' (or father's) class. . .[17]

Some authors have taken class as their unit for studying mobility although the subject has not been raised recently.[18] Studies of historical and crosssectional types attempt to analyze the association between mobility, class, and class structure formation.[19] The results of these studies are somewhat similar to the study of occupational mobility. "There appears to be a great deal of similarity in class mobility among these capitalist contexts taking into account their different class structures."[20] According to the same cited study, it also appears that "early industrial capitalist and contemporary Third World capitalist societies. . . were expected to have high rates of class mobility. In contrast advanced industrial capitalist societies. . . were expected to have low rates of mobility."[21] It may also be proposed here in this connection that rates of class mobility tend to decrease throughout the development of a capitalist formation. In Israel it is likely that class mobility decreased over the years mainly because of the waning effect of those structural factors such as immigration and the growing consolidation of the class structure.

There is hardly any information on class mobility in Israel. The literature takes socioeconomic factors such as education as ingredients of mobility while regarding status or prestige as units of social positions.[22] Information on occupational mobility specifies certain conditions such as the enforced changes that newcomers encountered.[23] As already reported, more than 60% of the newcomers in the 1950s and 1960s had to change their occupation after immigration. Moreover, reviewing the general trend of change it seems that about 50% of the changers became proletariat engaging in agriculture as wage laborers or in industry and services. This point is analyzed in more rigorous fashion in Chapter 7. Other studies of occupational mobility in Israel specify the effects of ethnic origin on opportunities of mobility, structural changes in the 1960s and 1970s on occupational mobility, and ethnicity-cum-year of immigration on occupational mobility.[24] Ethnicity and education had a decisive and differential effect; Ashkenazim had less need to change their occupations from what they had previously been than did Sephardim. The mobility of Israeli-born Ashkenazim was better than that of Israeli-born Sephardim.[25] Education assisted both groups to move up, but since education is an acquired asset, the opportunities gap in the process of status attainment already starts in school.[26] Even in the 1980s Sephardim were less likely to improve their class position than Ashkenazim. As already shown both groups proved resilient but Ashkenazim did better than Sephardim.

Very little evidence is needed here to support the proposition that minorities experience less upward mobility than the hegemonic group. Despite the example of the Jews in the the United States, religious or cultural factors influence the actual possibilities of mobility.[27] This is a structural factor in capitalist societies where one finds that the socioeconomic system is divided along political/cultural boundaries or the market is split along ethnic group lines deterring mobility. The opportunities for Israeli Arabs, for example, to move up in the class structure seem comparatively limited.

In this chapter class structure mobility analysis is carried out for ethnic origin, religion, and gender. These factors have also been used in the previous chapters because they, more than others specified in this study, may constitute alternative bases for the emergence of processes competing with class structure formation. The relevance and impact of these factors to the study of mobility in general and class mobility in particular is obvious.

The present analysis of class mobility uses the odd-ratio procedure. The units of analysis are classes and three other social categories; ethnicity, gender, and religion. Mobility of class is therefore tested in association with the other categories. The procedure of calculating the odds of mobility is simply and productively based on two by two tables.[28] The first one deals with Sephardim vs. others (Ashkenazim + Israeli-born) for 1961 vs. 1972, and then 1972 vs. 1983.

The division here between Sephardim and others is intentional. It is the interest of this part of the study to examine the attainments of those categories that are considered minorities not because of their size (although possibly an influential factor) but because they constitute certain social characteristics that may affect the process of class position allocation.

There are some advantages to the measure that is utilized here; the most important is that it treats the odds of social-mobility net of the overall marginal distribution of class positions. It treats the associations between certain variables that may be obscured by the different sizes of classes over the periods or by other interfering factors.[29] It is thus possible to assess the effects of certain structural characteristics beside that of class on the relative chances of individuals of different ethnic or other categorical characteristics to improve class position or to maintain it.[30] The odds ratios that are derived by cross-classification of class with these characteristics provide information on competition between different ethnicities, genders, or religions vs. classes on the individual's chances of obtaining a particular class position.

The odds-ratio is acknowledged to be a good measure of association and is used here although some drawbacks should be noted. The advantages of this measure make it highly productive despite the defects cited in the literature.[31] The outcome of calculating odds is straightforward; the closer the value of an odds ratio to unity the more perfect is the mobility and the less is the association between mobility, class, ethnicity or other characteristics as selected for comparison in the particular case under examination. Logged-odds ratio which is also used here indicates the relative in-mobility of the group first listed in the comparison. A negative value indicates larger in-mobility of this group. This provides further information for interpretation of odds of mobility regarding the compared groups.

The following are sets of odds ratios of class mobility by ethnicity, gender, and religion. Derivation is conducted for two separate periods: 1961 to 1972, and 1972 to 1983. In each pair the above three components are assessed.

Entries in the cells of Table 6.1 are odds ratios of the association between ethnic origin and relative mobility between class positions. Inspection of the relevant information indicates the different association between ethnic origin and class position at a certain period, and also the changes over time. Logged odds-ratios assist in interpretation of the results; negative values indicate a larger relative in-mobility of the category/group listed first in the contrast while positive values appear when the opposite occurs. Values close to zero mean that mobility for the two compared groups is similar.[32]

Table 6.1. Relative Mobility within Classes: Odds Ratios; Sephardim vs. Others;*
1961-1972 and 1972-1983

Period	1961–1972		1972–1983	
	Odds Ratio	Logged-Odds Ratio	Odds Ratio	Logged-Odds Ratio
Class				
1	.175	-1.742	.902	-.103
2	.679	-.387	.466	-.763
3	.666	-.406	.511	-.671
4	.536	-.623	1.290	.254
5	.646	-.436	1.002	.003

* See explanation in the following text. Others refers to Ashkenazim and Israeli-born.

The interpretation of the data in Table 6.1 is thus quite straightforward. The Sephardim group is listed first in the comparison. It appears that the period of 1961 to 1972 was highly unequal regarding Class 1 and less so for other classes. But still the odds ratios indicate inequality in favor of others. The logged-odds ratios add important information: in all of the classes in this period the in-mobility of Sephardim was substantive and relatively more then that of others. This is anticipated by the information presented in the preceding analysis of class-cum-ethnic formulation and by the general information on the development of the Israeli society during the first decade; immigration from Asia and Africa in the second half of this period was predominant and thus immigrants of this origin entered the economy in both absolute terms and relative proportion to others, mainly toward the 1960s when the mobility of Asia/Africa immigrants increased. The odds ratios of the following period are significant; there is almost equal mobility regarding Class 1 and Class 5. The logged-odds ratios are still in favor of Sephardim in-mobility into the first three classes but not into the last two. The process of proletarization of the Sephardim was exhausted during the 1970s. The latter's fate was influenced by the growing number of Arabs from the occupied territories in the Israeli economy particularly in the proletariat.

Table 6.2. Relative Mobility within Classes: Odds Ratios; Males vs. Females;
1961-1972, 1972-1983

Period	1961–1972		1972–1983	
	Odds Ratio	Logged-Odds Ratio	Odds Ratio	Logged-Odds Ratio
Class				
1	.894	-.112	4.830	.574
2	1.054	.052	.930	-.072
3	1.017	.016	1.146	.136
4	1.775	.573	1.440	.364
5	.953	-.048	1.260	.231

In three out of the five classes in the 1961-1972 period the odds indicate that mobility chances were virtually indifferent to gender (odds close to unity). But in Class 1 the in-mobility of men (this group is listed first in the comparison) was larger. The logged value in Class 5 is close to zero and thus it appears that the in- or out-mobility of both gender groups was similar. In this period the in-mobility of women regarding Class 4 increased. In the second period three out of five odds increased. Classes 1, 3, and 5 and although decreasing slightly were still above unity regarding Class 4. In all but Class 2 the in-mobility of women improved and was quite substantial in Class 1. All in all, the odds of women (listed second in the comparison) improved during the years (see logged-odds) apparently regardless of the effects of certain structural changes. It should be remembered that the odds ratio assesses the relative chances of mobility of a member of a certain category over a period of time while ignoring structural changes like an increase in the size of a certain class, or in the labor force and so on. In this study Jewish and Arab women are treated as one group despite the considerable evidence that the odds of gender-cum-religion were different regarding Jews and Arabs and more particularly for females. The religious factor's effect on class mobility is assessed below.

As already noted, the Arab minority in Israel was integrated into the Israeli economy in the late 1950s and early 1960s. The Arabs were and remained a distinct social minority for both economic and political reasons. They were integrated into the Israeli economy at quite an accelerated pace and constituted a potential and actual proletariat. One has to be aware of the possibility of a split market or more precisely, two markets in relation to the Arab population. Besides the economic instance of the Israeli society the Arabs maintain a sectoral/enclave economy. Thus a capitalist employer of Arab descent may only employ Arabs.

This is not new. Jews in the the United States in the early years of this century ran a similar type of sectoral economy as they had done already in Russia in the second half of the nineteenth. century.[33] Other evidence points to the recent immigration of Central Americans who entered the the United States economy through that enclave's sectoral economy.[34]

Table 6.3. Relative Mobility within Classes: Odds Ratios; Jews and Arabs; 1961-1972, 1972-1983

Period	1961–1972		1972–1983	
	Odds Ratio	Logged-Odds Ratio	Odds Ratio	Logged-Odds Ratio
Class/				
1	(—*)	(—*)	.870	-.139
2	.813	-.202	1.206	.187
3	.990	.010	3.237	1.174
4	1.801	.588	1.596	.467
5	1.380	.322	2.085	.734

* Not executed because of empty cell for Arabs in 1961.

Odds by religion in 1961–1972 changed in relative terms in Classes 4 and 5 where Arab in-mobility was clearly indicated (positive sign in the logged-odds ratios). In the second period, 1972–1983, odds of mobility by religion continued to change with more open class boundaries. In four out of the five classes in-mobility of Arabs was evident. This time Class 1 became closed while Class 3, managers, supervisors, and professionals, became more open to the Arabs as did Class 5. In terms of mobility and several other indicators Israeli Arabs improved their position throughout the period. They enjoyed, however, less improvement than did the Jewish population. Some of this gap can be attributed to structural conditions such as the high percentage of Arabs in agriculture at the beginning of the period, their level of education, and so forth. Some can be attributed to the policy of the Israeli government while some was caused by the structural changes that affected the entire Israeli society.

The above indices distinguish structural (or forced or demand) mobility from exchange (or pure or "circulation" mobility). Structural mobility is that part of the total observed mobility that is directly caused by changes in the structure of society, that is, in the objective conditions that enhance or deter class structure formation and, correlatively, class mobility. This is important for this study that has an eventual interest in the structural conditions which have shaped the class structure since the establishment of the state. An attendant procedure called "disparity ratios" offers a simple formula to assess the magnitude of the effects of the structural factors.[35] This ratio is used to assess the effects of changes in the structure of objective mobility opportunities in the studied preiod on the chances of individuals by gender, ethnicity, and origin of religion.

The immediate question to be asked concerns the structural changes during the period 1948–1983. What happened to the opportunities of these categories? This procedure is carried out practically by using the distribution of individuals in class positions in two consecutive periods as before: 1961–1972 and 1972–1983. The first period in a pair is considered here as the comparative point of departure. As before odd values indicate the chances of an individual of a certain category and class at a

Table 6.4. Disparity Ratios: Ethnic Origin, Gender, and Religion: 1961-72, 1972-83

Period	1961–1972		1972–1983	
	Ethnic Origin*			
	Seph.	Ashk.	Seph.	Ashk.
Class				
1	4.435	.775	1.076	.971
2	1.672	.854	2.308	.641
3	1.418	.948	2.418	.824
4	2.988	.840	2.104	.940
5	1.250	.819	1.266	.812
	Gender			
	Male	Female	Male	Female
Class				
1	1.002	.874	.937	4.588
2	.988	1.047	1.015	.939
3	.993	1.259	.951	1.072
4	.808	1.414	.828	1.214
5	1.062	.962	.954	1.205
	Religion			
	Jewish	Others	Jewish	Others
Class				
1	.984	(—)**	1.004	.914
2	.939	.829	.984	1.179
3	1.000	1.000	.958	3.157
4	.983	1.750	.979	1.571
5	.983	1.346	.897	1.876

*   Ashkenazim.
** See footnote, Table 6.3.
     Seph. = Sephardim, Ashk. = Ashkenazim

whether or not the changes in the size and composition of class positions during the above compared (sub) periods had any impact on the chances of individuals from definite social categories as presented in Table 6.4.

The structural effects operating in the two periods had some influence on class mobility; that is, the increase and changes in the positions of classes improved the chances of the minorities. The increase in the share of the Sephardim in the labor market in both periods apparently had an effect on Sephardi chances of mobility to all five classes compared to that of the Ashkenazim whose share in the labor market decreased. However, it must be noted again that the disparity ratios do not specify the exact component of the structure that was in effect but points to the fact that structural changes had a concrete influence on class-cum-ethnic association (or other social categories) treated here concerning practical odds of mobility.

Structural changes also had effects on women's chances of class mobility; these chances continued to be "in favor" in the second period, but except in Classes 1 and 5 the size of the ratio decreased. The changes in female class mobility can be attributed in part to the increase of female participation in the labor force.

The class mobility of others (essentially Arabs) compared to Jews was also affected by the structural changes. More Arabs joined the labor force and more entered the Jewish sector of the economy. Chances of mobility grew in regard to Classes 4 and 5 (the semiautonomous and the proletariat), but they also grew in regard of Class 3, managers, supervisors, and so on. It is difficult to decide here which was the main cause that determined chances of mobility in regard of this social category. Other sources suggest twin tracks for Arab mobility;[36] Israeli Arabs indeed improved their class positions, but less than did the Jews. The 1967 war had more then a minor effect on Israeli Arabs; the noncitizen Arabs then began to replace them in the lower positions in the class structure, and in the less-favored positions within the proletariat.

The effects of structural conditions on the class structure of Israeli society have already been observed at the outset of this study. Immigration was suggested as a major cause. Other potential factors that may explain the changes in the class structure over the period have also been considered. It now appears that the composition of the immigration—the greater proportion of immigrants from Asia and Africa—affected the composition of different classes, and correlatively, the chances of individuals from these countries of origin to be assigned to a certain class. The growth in the number of females in the labor force was another factor associated with class mobility odds. The opening of the Jewish market and other factors affected the chances of the Arabs. Thus the ratios derived from assessing relative mobility in odds terms of "exchange" and "forced" mobility indicate that the class structure in Israel started as approximating a closed system in which the Jewish veteran Ashkenazi male population dominated, and then was forced to open to the new social categories. However, this was a differential openness of the class structure; in some classes the in-mobility of certain social categories was higher than in others.

The effect of immigration on class mobility and on the class composition had two stages, immediate and delayed. The immediate effect was the entrance of immigrants into positions in the labor market, conditioned by the economic opportunities at the time of immigration. Individuals having certain qualities had a better chance than those who did not, but they were limited by the encountered socioeconomy and class structure. It was far less refined than in other countries where the capitalist system emerged within a historical continuity. The proletariat was composed of more individuals from a certain origin than others, and actually many started in this class just because of the lack of other alternatives, although they had some qualifications that would had helped them to attain better class positions under better socioeconomic conditions.

The immediate effect of immigration was evident through an examination of the class-cum-immigration effect. Inspection of cross-classification of class positions in 1961 compared to class positions before emigration (a slightly different sampling because only individuals who were in class positions before emigration are considered here for assessing change in class position), shows that many of the immigrants at that time had to change their class positions. A good 40% of the male immigrants changed class position although a higher proportion of Sephardim than Ashkenazim became proletariat.[37] A similar picture with different quantitative values was repeated in 1972 and again in 1983.

The delayed effect was evident in the ethnic-cum-education combination; after graduating from the Israeli school system, the children of the immigrants entered the economic system, and should have affected the combination of the class structure by reducing the effect of the ethnic factor. As recent studies show, the educational system indeed had concrete influence on individual attainment in the economy and on the class position of these individuals, but this was a differential effect; ethnic origin made its stamp on achievement in education and attainments in the economy. Among the second generation of immigrants who were raised in Israel, the sons of Sephardim did worse than their Ashkenazi colleagues. The delayed effect could be observed also within the female population, in their growing share in the labor market and so forth. Despite all these effects, the class structure combination was affected by the improvement of certain qualities within certain social categories. This had an impact on the distribution of the basic classes and the contradictory locations, and on the internal composition of these classes.

Both forced and exchange mobility were prominent in the studied period, and both had an impact on class positions reallocation. As already noted, this study contends that structural conditions and structural changes determined the format of the class structure and the extent of mobility opportunities. Some students of this subject suggest technical procedures to deal with the relative and distinct effects of structural and of exchange mobility in a certain society over time, and even to determine the relations between a particular change in the social structure and change(s) in the pattern of mobility.[38] Such procedures are not reproduced here, but it is still suggested that class mobility as well as class structure formulation are primarily the effects of structural factors, of what happened in the economy and in society, and of the degree of openness of the class system that is determined by the conjuncture's needs. Though not elaborated here, class mobility is also influenced by intervention of different agents who compete over the formation of "class system and/or other forms of collectivities." The process described below lends some support to this.

> There was, by now, an immigrant Jewish proletariate of considerable
> size in the American cities, a proletariate intensively exploited and
> inclined every few years to outbursts of extreme discontent.[39]

Perhaps the most important outcome of immigration is the process of "becoming proletariat." Proletarization indicates a process (or already a position) by which an individual becomes a part of the labor process and sells his labor in the economic market, since this is the only asset he possesses.[40] A position of proletariat assumes no control over capital, labor force, or labor processes.

Proletarization arises through two major possible avenues: transformation of mode of production—as when a capitalist replaces a feudal mode, or through immigration from one country to another, and in certain conditions even between regions within the same country.[41] Immigrants encounter a class system to which they have to readjust.[42] Yet mass immigration affects the class structure itself, changing the composition of classes, perhaps adding some positions of contradictory locations, and in the long run, being a main reason for the modifications in the socioeconomic system. The development of the economy, politics and other institutions of Israeli society made it necessary to rearrange the class structure between and within classes; the growth of industry could not be attained without a proper increase in the working class. So it was with labor for public and personal services. The result was the emergence of a proletariat.

This society had experienced proletarization before. However, for social and historical reasons, this had been different from the present experience.[43] A relatively class-conscious proletariat of the prestate period was now replaced by a reluctant proletariat. The difference between pre- and poststate immigration also occurred in the process of proletarization; poststate, it occurred within a mass immigration, with an increasing proportion of immigrants from underdeveloped countries (primarily semifeudalistic). The latter had very little, if any, experience in modern industry or more inclusive experience in capitalist formulation. The majority of the immigrants from Asia and Africa imported to Israel different "conditions of production"; that is, the level of socioeconomic development of their countries of emigration was in general lower then that of Europe and America, and also lower than Israel.[44]

As with other processes of social formation, there are common features to the process of proletarization everywhere, but it also differs from one country to another. The extent of variability is determined by social and historical conditions. In Israel after statehood the mere fact of mass immigration into a small-scale economy that had almost no domestic resources affected the pace and extent of the process of proletarization, the chances of remaining in this class after immigration, and the opportunities of "redemption." In essence, the encounter between imported and existing conditions of production determined structural conditions for the emergence of a proletariat and its size. Nonetheless, the particular attainment of a class position was determined by other factors such as the qualities of the individual and the particular needs of the economy at the point of immigration.

On very few historical occasions have immigrants had the opportunity or power to be engaged in the transformation of the class system within which they were located. This happened in the United States during the eighteenth and nineteenth centuries, as well as at the begining of this century.[45] The same process is occurring in a very specific manner in Europe of today, where immigrants (such as Gastarbieter) are changing the composition of the proletariat in certain European countries and forcing it to be divided along ethnic lines. This is accompanied by the rearrangement of the class structure, since it is inevitable that no single class in a class structure can be totally autonomous and other classes thus respond to the former's reorganization.

The situation in Israel in the first decade of statehood and thereafter had a comprehensive effect upon the immigrants. It forced many to change occupation, class, political ties, and social nets. The influence of the structure and its specific content has already been dealt with; the size of the proletariat had decreased by the 1980s. This was the product of changes in the economy, politics, and so forth. This means also that the chances of an individual member of society entering, remaining in, or leaving the proletariat were lower then before. Yet the question remains, what factors still determined the chances of individuals or what factors constituted the process of allocation to class position; which one or ones can be considered responsible for proletarization?

The variables used here to investigate the process of proletarization have already been used in an other ways during examination of the process of allocation to class positions. These are gender, age, ethnic origin, religion, year of immigration, and education. The procedure used here is that of Probit that "can be used to estimate the effects of one or more independent variables on a dichotomous dependent variable."[46] This makes it possible to treat the process of becoming proletariat separately from the overall process of allocation to the class structure.

In order to treat a Probit model of proletarization the five-class structure in this study was collapsed into two; the proletariat, Class 5, and the other Classes (1 to 4) together. The exogenous variables have been dichotomized as in earlier tables. The results of the procedure are shown in Table 6.5 .

Table 6.5. Probit Model of Proletariat vs. Others by Six Independent Variables:
1961, 1972, 1983

Year/ Variables	1961	1972	1983
Gender	-1.052*	-1.286*	-1.293*
Age	-0.678*	-0.860*	-1.002*
Ethnic Origin	-1.672*	-1.302*	-1.148*
Year of Immigration	1.145*	0.997*	0.695*
Education	-4.332*	-3.407*	-2.955*
Religion**	1.680*	-1.302*	2.680*
Intercept	5.240*	5.530*	5.447*
P ***	.009	.000	.000

*   Z-value equal to or greater than 2.
**   Because of some technicalities, this variable's coefficient in 1983 is warranted.
*** Pearson Goodness-of-Fit. Missing values in this procedure are excluded. An
      independent test of the same model but including missing values provided the
      same relative sizes of coefficients.

The coefficients in Table 6.5 are interpreted following the prime characteristics
attributed to Probit coefficients; they indicate the change in probability of becoming
(or remaining) proletariat vs. others, resulting from a unit change in the independent variable under discussion.[47] The size of the coefficient reflects this probability, although the pure probability itself should be calculated in addition to
the coefficients estimation. Here it is sufficient to infer effects from coefficients as
they are presented in the table. Note that the dependent variable—proletarization—refers both to individuals who became proletariat immediately after
immigration or some time later, and also to those who became proletariat but were
born in Israel. These different groups are not treated separately.

Judging by the size of the coefficients it appears that the variables can be ordered
by their contribution to the probability of becoming proletariat in the three
consecutive periods as follows:

1961 = Education, Religion, Ethnic Origin, Immigration Year, Gender, Age.
1972 = Education, Religion, Ethnic Origin, Gender, Immigration Year, Age.
1983 = Education, Religion, Gender, Ethnic Origin, Age, Immigration Year.

Time makes some changes, but they are not very pronounced. Actually some
pattern is observed; education, religion, gender or ethnic origin were the most
relative effective factors regarding the probability of becoming proletariat. Consi-

dering the way these variables were dichotomised for this model, it then appears that an educated, Jewish, Ashkenazi female is likely to be immune from becoming proletariat. Thus the process of becoming proletariat centered on acquired or imported assets of education and being assigned to a definite minority group. But this group had differing effects; being a woman increased the likelihood of not becoming proletariat, while being a Sephardi increased this likelihood. The correlation between these variables was not tested here but forms a first-hand source.[48] From other sources it is evident that the likelihood of a Sephardi woman becoming proletariat is higher than for an Ashkenazi woman. As for the effect of religion, this needs no more elaboration. It is deduced that the lot of the non-Jews is less favorable.

One other point is worth repeating. Year of immigration had the expected effect with the size of the coefficients decreasing from 1961 to 1983. Additional inspection of the interaction between this variable and others in this equation indicates that year of immigration was correlated to ethnic origin in 1961 (the only substantial coefficient at that time), to ethnic origin in 1972 (correlation with religion is redundant since non-Jews never immigrated), and to ethnic origin and education in 1983. The size of the correlation coefficients with ethnic origin was decreasing during the entire period, indicating the change of size and combination of immigration waves.

The likelihood of becoming proletariat was and still is influenced by the assets of the individual. But the concrete possibilities are determined by structural factors— the real changes that occur in the economy and social composition of the society and so on. Thus when the number of persons employed in the agricultural sector is decreased and when industry becomes more sophisticated and expands the less manual positions, the size of the proletariat shrinks. This is a slightly more complex process since the correlation between position in agriculture and industry and the proletariat positions is not unity. But primarily this is the proper description of the association between changes in the major instances of society and the likeliehood of becoming proletariat.

To some extent it was possible to assess the effect of the conditions of production in the country of emigration and the likelihood of becoming proletariat. Recalling the drawbacks of the ethnic origin factor (two general/gross categories with a lot of internal variability), the 1961 census data made it possible to test the effect of imported conditions of production as it refers to the country of emigration's socioeconomic level of development. This was excuted in the 1961 sample only.

This period was selected because the labor force then included many newcomers who either entered the labor market almost immediately after immigration, or who matured through school but themselves were born outside Israel and immigrated after the age of fourteen, and whose major socialization took place before immigration.[49]

Each country of emigration was assigned a GNP score, a substitute for conditions of production.[50] The same Probit model was rerun, but this time with another variable—the GNP of the country of emigration. This variable's contribution to the likelihood of becoming proletariat is positive and significant, indicating a greater likelihood of immigrants from lower GNP countries becoming proletariat than others. But this variable eliminates the variable of ethnic origin; when the GNP is inserted into the equation, ethnic origin becomes insignificant in size and probability. In other words, the GNP variable made a direct contribution to the likelihood of becoming proletariat, while ethnic origin did not. This supports the contention that the fate of the immigrants is partly determined by some suprastructural factors. The encounter between imported and existing conditions *cetaris paribus* at a specific period of immigration influenced the process of allocation to class positions of proletariat as well as of other classes.

The information on mobility since 1948 presented in this chapter relates the subject to the structural conditions: first, the class structure since 1948 has become more open regarding definite social categories; neither ethnicity, gender, nor even religion has constituted a rigid buffer to class mobilization. But still they have had more then some effect on mobility. Second, structural changes in the society directly affected the realm of opportunities. Hence a change in the composition of the labor force, or of industry had a direct effect on the process of allocation to proletarian class positions. An individual's assets such as education were highly important in determining his class position and his chances of mobility between class positions, but it should be remembered that structure comes first, at least when mobility and related issues are considered.

The mobility within classes during the three subperiods discussed here, as well as the process of proletarization, reflects the undergoing process of structural changes in the economy, politics, and other instances of Israeli society. Class structure was changing because of the changing socioeconomic factors and the growing process of transformation toward a capitalist system. Hence, the observed ratios of mobility and the observed determinants of proletarization enjoy only a relative autonomy in passing on information on the society. They are directly or indirectly the outcomes of the major events that occured in the structure of the Israeli society.

NOTES

1. This is indeed the unit of analysis which is specified by the "status attainment" study. See Note 1 to Chapter 5.
2. This is the major thesis of some studies of mobility in capitalist/industrial societies. It is adopted by status-attainment approach and by the open-society approach. See Goldthorpe discussion in Chapter 1 of his book, 1980.
3. Lipset and Zetterberg,1959; Hauser et al., 1975; Hauser and Featherman, 1977; Erikson, Goldthorpe et al., 1982.
4. Erikson et al., 1982.
5. Goldthorpe, 1980; Hauser Dickinson et al., 1975; Duncan, 1966.

6. Bonachic, 1976; Kelenberg and Sorensen; 1979; also Beck et al., 1978; Piory, 1975.
7. Goldthorpe, 1980.
8. Goldthorpe, 1980.
9. Goldthorpe, 1980.
10. Hauser et al., 1975; Simkus, 1984.
11. Simkus, 1984.
12. Robinson, 1984.
13. Simkus, 1984.
14. Wright, 1978, 1982. Also Ehrenreich and Ehrenreich, 1971.
15. Robinson, 1984.
16. Robinson, 1984; Goldthorpe, 1980.
17. Hauser et al., 1975.
18. Robinson, 1984; Goldthorpe, 1980; Wright, 1982.
19. Aminzade and Hodson, 1982.
20. Robinson, 1984.
21. Robinson, 1984.
22. Adler and Hodge, 1973; Kraus, 1982; Tyree 1981. Also Hodge, 1973.
23. Sicron, 1957; Halevi and Klinov-Malul, 1968; Matras, 1965; Matras, Noam and Bar-Haim, 1984.
24. Ben-Porath, 1986. Also Kraus, 1982; Smoocha, 1978.
25. Ben-Porath, 1986.
26. Matras, et al., 1984.
27. Liberson, 1970; Hodge, 1973; Lewin-Epstein and Semyonov, 1986.
28. Aminzade and Hodson, 1982.
29. Goldthorpe, 1980.
30. Simpson et al., 1982; Tyree, 1973.
31. Tyree, 1981.
32. Lewin-Epstein and Semyonov, 1986.
33. Howe, 1976. Jews were engaged in a closed ethnic economy in Russia after 1861. This was culturally bounded because of the religious restrictions on working on the Sabbath, and so forth. In the United States this was only temporary and covered only a fraction of the Jewish immigrants. Ben-Porat, 1986-87.
34. Portes and Stepnick, 1985.
35. Goldthorpe, 1980.
36. Ben-Porath, 1986; Smoocha, 1978; Lewin-Epstein and Semyonov, 1986.
37. Ben-Porat, 1987.
38. Goldthorpe, 1980; Hauser et al., 1975.
39. Howe, 1976.
40. Aminzade and Hodson, 1982; Braverman, 1974; Merriman, 1979; Tilly, 1983; Ben-Porat, 1987.
41. Castels and Kosack, 1973; Piory, 1979.
42. Ben-Porat, 1987.

43. Ben-Porat, 1986.
44. Taylor and Hudson, 1972.
45. Bodnar, 1977; Rosenblum, 1973.
46. SPSSX, 1986.
47. Peterson, 1985.
48. Ben-Porat, 1987a.
49. Hartman, 1981.
50. Gorin, 1984.

7

Structural Transformation:
Class and Sector

The relatively short history of the Israeli state unfolds as one long process of transformation; organizations, social categories, institutions and the state itself underwent changes that had real qualitative outcomes. Indeed this is what is anticipated from a process toward capitalization; at the higher level of abstraction one inspects the correspondance between the economic instance and those of politics and so forth, and the emerging new rules of structural determination, that is, the weakening of the limiting ties between politics and economy and the accompanied strengthening of the economy. At a lower level of abstraction one inspects the changes in the variables of the social structure and their correlation with such other changes as in the composition of labor force, in quality of education and its distribution, in reorganization of sectors and branches of the economy, in political rules of industrial relations, and so forth.

Most important is the change that occurs in the organization of production, although it is among the least explicit. Students of development and growth of societies usually treat outcomes of change as if they signify the rearranging the face of society including its institutions and so forth. But very few dare to take a further step. Sociologists who deal with matrices of intergenerational mobility of occupation are probably more aware of the hidden influence of structural factors on the form and rate of mobility. This is examined through the identification of intermediate variables, that connect between structure and behaviour. If one departs from the structural limitation of the socioeconomic formation, one at least dares to specify mode of causality, that is, dares to proceed beyond merely describing "what happened" to the prime ingredients of the structure, to the explanation of changes or modifications in the observed behavior of forms of society; hence, to questions of "why" and "how".

It is often contended by students—although with little agreement on conceptuali-zation—that changes in political institutions may induce changes in other instances of society including the economy, and correlatively, industry and services. The perspective adopted here endorses this to a degree; the ability of politics to change the economy is determined by the economy itself. At a certain point the political influence on the economy comes to an impasse and any further change implies a necessary transformation in the economic level. But it is possible that politics may predominate in formulating economic behavior and through this behavior reshape the class structure. For instance, a new policy of capital investments may enforce redistribution of class positions in certain sectors of industry.

As previously noted, one has to be aware of the distinction between the factors that affect the recruitment to and/or redistribution of positions of class and those factors that impose a qualitative change of the class structure. The latter is associ-ated with critical change in the organization of production, with new rules of organizing the process of production and the relationships between the major parti-cipating categories. This may lead to a new order of the class structure, such as new basic classes. However, organization of production can be affected by less dramatic changes. It can be affected by investment policy, by certain technological progress, or by changes in and between sectors of the economy. This may lead to redistribution of the existing positions of class or to some modification, while retaining the basic rules of correspondence between class structure and the positions in the economy. The big change in countries moving toward capitalism is related, sometimes causally, to the transformation of the mode of production. The move within industry to greater automation or the increase in the share of services at the expense of industry, is less dramatic in its effect on society. Nevertheless, it may lead to redistribution or reallocation of individuals into class positions. This must be studied in order to decide on the possible outcome of minor changes. The meaning of changes in the proportion of positions between basic and contradictory classes, the ups and downs of certain classes like the petty-bourgeoisie in a capitalist society, or the emergence of a new middle class is equivocal. But it can be certainly stated that these are the effects of more basic structural changes that influence the form and content of the class structure.

This study is concerned with the structure of the class system and the structural factors that enhance its creation and modification. Some of the major causes of changes in the whole society were introduced in the first chapter. Obviously these changes had at least some effect on the class structure during the four decades since statehood.

A further analysis of an assumed correspondence between the structure of the socioeconomical system and the stability or degree of change of the class structure follows.

Table 7.1. Class Structure by Sectors of the Economy: 1961, 1972, 1983 (Percentages)

Class/Sector* & Year		1	2	3	4	5	Total
	1961	.6	44.0	1.3	3.1	51.0	100.0
1	1972	1.7	53.4	1.7	11.2	31.9	100.0
	1983	1.9	50.9	9.4	8.5	29.2	100.0
	1961	1.7	19.8	6.9	6.0	65.6	100.0
2	1972	2.6	11.0	12.1	14.6	62.1	100.0
	1983	2.2	9.0	15.4	21.4	52.0	100.0
	1961	2.8	8.3	—	—	88.9	100.0
3	1972	—	—	20.0	23.3	56.7	100.0
	1983	—	—	34.0	30.0	36.0	100.0
	1961	1.0	14.9	6.5	7.5	70.0	100.0
4	1972	4.6	15.4	5.4	12.0	62.5	100.0
	1983	3.9	13.8	5.0	19.9	57.5	100.0
	1961	—	1.9	11.1	18.5	68.5	100.0
5	1972	1.9	48.8	3.8	35.8	9.7	100.0
	1983	3.6	28.2	11.7	45.5	10.9	100.0
	1961	2.9	42.0	7.2	19.6	28.3	100.0
6	1972	1.8	13.7	10.6	29.1	44.9	100.0
	1983	.5	12.6	14.8	31.3	40.7	100.0
	1961	—	46.2	6.4	24.4	23.1	100.0
7	1972	2.5	13.0	25.0	53.5	6.0	100.0
	1983	3.7	11.2	23.9	56.8	4.3	100.0
	1961	2.5	13.0	49.4	24.4	10.8	100.0
8	1972	.3	4.6	56.1	19.4	19.6	100.0
	1983	—	2.8	51.0	31.3	15.0	100.0
	1961	—	17.1	5.1	12.0	65.8	100.0
9	1972	2.5	33.5	8.1	14.9	41.0	100.0
	1983	2.8	18.9	17.2	16.1	45.0	100.0

* Sectors defined here following the CBS code are:
1—agriculture, forestry and fishing; 2—industry (mining and manufacturing); 3—electricity and water; 4—construction (building and public works); 5—commerce, restaurants and hotels; 6—transport, storage and communication; 7—financing and business services; 8—public and community services; 9—personal and other services.

What are the possible effects of the changes in sectors of the economy on the reshaping of the classes in Israeli society? It is worth noting that the changes in the sectors of the economy constitute a "second-order" cause; they themselves are the results of more basic changes in the organization of production, such as the move from agriculture to industry and services. The essence here is qualitative; industry produces more positions of authority and of expertise than agriculture and demands other qualifications. The growth of services also affects the composition of class positions. Thus the move from agriculture into industry may change the internal composition of the working class. The move from industry to services, however one defines the latter, may increase the positions in contradictory locations, enhancing the emergence of the "new bourgeoisie". This move may increase the share of the state in the labor process, and so forth.

The strategy employed here is intended to decompose the total changes in the sectors of the economy into two components: first, the industry-shift effect that assesses the changes in the class structure due to changes in overall sectoral distribution or distribution of the labor force across industries/sectors between time periods; second, the class-composition effect that assesses the changes in class structure due to the changes within a given industry/sector over the same pairs of periods. Further clarification is provided later.

-The class structure by sectors already indicates changes through the overall period; Class 1 has changed little by sector—the percentage increased by some fractions of a point, but it reached only 4.6% in the construction sector where many employers/contractors were located in the 1970s. Prominent changes are observed in Class 2, the petty-bourgeoisie, and Class 3, managers and professionals. Changes are also very obvious in Classes 4 and 5 during the whole period. These fluctuations should be warranted however, since they are derived from sample(s) and not directly from the cross-classification of the population at large. They are, however, in accordance with the changes in class structure over the three specified periods. Table 7.2 is a reminder of the changes in the class structure.

Table 7.2. Class Structure: 1961, 1972, 1983; and Changes between 1961 and 1972, and between 1972 and 1983

Class/Year and Percent of Change	1961	1972	% Change	1983	%Change
Class					
1	1.5	2.0	-0.5	1.8	-0.2
2	22.5	19.3	-3.1	11.9	-7.5
3	15.6	19.7	4.1	26.6	6.9
4	13.1	22.9	9.8	30.1	7.2
5	47.4	36.0	-11.4	28.8	-7.2

Judging by the changes between the pairs of periods, 1961/1972 and 1972/1983, it seems that the changes of classes within sectors were indeed more critical. This is now tested in a more thorough manner.

The next step is to proceed with the analysis of the class-cum-sector effects throughout the entire period. They are the result of other preceding or simultaneous changes in the economy, politics, and so forth. Furthermore, in most of the historical cases, sectoral changes precede class structure changes. Thus it seems reasonable to state the causal relations between industry-sector changes and class structure modification. But this is not always true. In certain situations the class structure may induce changes in the sectors of the economy. This was evident when the first prestate waves of immigration reached Palestine[1] and also at the period of mass immigration after statehood, when the government reallocated individuals into class positions—through placement in the labor market—and was responsible for increasing the size of the agricultural sector. Later on it was also responsible for the increase in the industrial sector, most prominently in construction where the government itself was involved through its building companies and by financial support for nongovernmental organizations.

The strategy of analysis of class-cum-sector, is of decomposing/disaggregating structural changes into the following components: 1. a sector shift effect, 2. a class-composition shift effect, and 3. an interaction effect.[2] Following Wright's analysis, industrial shift refers to the changes in class structure that result from the changes in the overall sectoral distribution of the labor force across industries.[3] The decline of agriculture at the end of the 1950s and during the 1960s probably had some effect on the size of the proletariat in Israeli economy and its reallocation in the latter sectors. The class-composition shift effect refers to changes in the class structure that result from changes within given sector(s) of the economy, independent of changes in the relative size of these sectors. Hence, as before, the decline (in labor and capital) of agriculture because of substantive increase in productivity decreased its proletariat and increased the share of the petty-bourgeoisie (small employers or selfemployed) but not necessarily the absolute numbers of this class within this sector. Agriculture in Israel at the end of the 1960s and during the 1970s was characterized by small holders in Moshavim (farmers' villages) kibbutzim, and private owners in small towns (with seasonal daily employees, mainly noncitizen Arabs). The third estimated effect is attributed to the interaction between the first and the second effect. Thus two independent effects and one interaction are estimated.

The decomposition process was executed first for 1961 to 1972, and then for 1972 to 1983. For each comparison pair the three effects were calculated separately.

Tables 7.3 and 7.4 show the effects of class, industrial sector, and interaction. The procedure by which these results were obtained was based on sample information, and thus it is not possible to give the actual (absolute) numbers of growth or of decline.[4]

Table 7.3. Decomposition of Changes in the Class Structure: 1961 to 1972; Industry-
Sector, Class, and Interaction Effects (Percentages)*

Class	Industry shift effect	Class composition & interaction shift effect	Class shift effect	Industry & interaction shift effect
1	-21.0	121.0	35.0	65.0
2	90.0	10.0	17.0	83.0
3	27.0	73.0	-26.0	126.0
4	19.0	81.0	11.0	89.0
5	1.0	99.0	-3.0	103.0

* Total change may exceed 100%.

In the first compared pair (1961 to 1972) the effects of industry shift and class
shift provide no one consistent pattern of results. Class 1 was more affected in 1961–
1972 by the class composition shift than by the industry-sector shift. More particularly, industry shift decreased this class volume while the class shift increased
it. Class 2 was affected by industry-sector shift much more than by class composition
shift. Class 5, was affected very little by the independent effects of industry sector
and class composition. It was affected by interaction effects.

Table 7.4. Decomposition of Changes in the Class Structure: 1972 to 1983; Industry-
Sector, Class, and Interaction Effects (Percentages)*

Class	Industry shift effect	Class composition & interaction shift effect	Class shift effect	Industry & interaction shift effect
1	128.0	-28.0	557.0	457.0
2	36.0	64.0	-21.0	121.0
3	74.0	26.0	22.0	78.0
4	6.0	94.0	5.0	95.0
5	36.0	64.0	33.0	66.0

Total change may exceed 100%

Table 7.5. Decomposition of Changes in the Israeli Class Structure as a Percentage of the 1961 and 1972 Class Structure Populations

Class		Industry sector shift	Class shift	Interaction shift	Total net change
1	1961	-13.6	22.7	54.5	-63.6
	1972	-16.6	-72.2	101.7	-12.9
2	1961	-22.0	–4.0	5.0	-21.0
	1972	-17.0	10.3	-40.6	-47.3
3	1961	13.2	-12.8	48.6	49.1
	1972	31.5	9.2	1.9	42.6
4	1961	26.3	14.7	97.4	138.4
	1972	2.4	2.2	38.3	42.9
5	1961	0.001	1.4	-42.8	-44.3
	1972	-8.6	-8.0	-7.7	-24.3

The results of the second comparison (1972 to 1983) reveal only some closeness to the previous decomposition. Class 1 was highly affected by class composition shift. Class 2 was affected more by industry-sector shift. The decomposition of Class 3 was different however. This class was affected by industry-sector more than by class composition. Very little independent effects are discerned in Class 4, while the independent effects of sector and class regarding Class 5 are relatively substantial in the second period. Table 7.5 provides much more digestible information on the effects of sector and class as a percentage of the net change from 1961 to 1972.

The entries in Table 7.5 provide the three components of the net shift as percentages of the number of individuals in the class in 1961—the beginning of the first decade, and 1972—the beginning of the second decade. The net shift is calculated as the outcome of the actual number of individuals in a certain class minus the expected number. As already presented above, the effects of class and industry may operate in different ways, thus the total net change may exceed 100% because of an extreme gap or gaps between actual and expected distributions.

The information in Table 7.5 does not reveal some order or pattern in the data across classes. But it is possible to observe total changes in the class structure, class by class. Class 1 was influenced by class-composition shift more then by sector shift. The influence of these shifts on Classes 2 and 3 in both periods, was different from Class 1; here the effect of industry-sector was greater than the effect of class composition. Class 4, the semiautonomous employee, was influenced in the first period by the changes in the industry sector and also by that of class composition. This class was not overly affected by these shifts in the next period.

In a way not anticipated the working class seems not to be much influenced by industry-sector shift (there is evidence to the latter effect in 1972). This is in contrast to expectations since in the first and second periods agriculture was decimated. This can be explained by pointing to the increase in Class 4 between 1961 and 1972, and by the fact that the total change indicates that the proletariat was declining. The interaction effect that seems in this case the only substantive effect in the first period, can be read as indicating the industry-cum-class composition effect as an explanation of the changes in this class. Nonetheless, it should be stated again that the fate of the Israeli proletariat was and still is related to the influx of Arab labor from the occupied territories. Hence it is possible to suggest here that the status of the Israeli proletariat was contingent on the increasing number of non-Israeli Arabs who joined the lower ranks of the economy, possibly effecting a reshaping of the proletariat. In other words, the modification of the industrial sectors and that of certain classes can be attributed to political as well as economic reasons.

Industrial sector reflects here a structural factor that determines the volume, distribution, and shift of class positions. Thus the fact that any single class and the whole structure of classes can be induced by factors such as sectoral industry and its development is anticipated. This was the case in Israeli society as well. But because of the peculiarity of the social structure, a point reiterated in this book, the association between the class structure of a single class, and changes in the major instances of the entire society was erratic. However, it appears that changes in the industrial sectors—probably caused by what happened in the fluctuating development of the society's socioeconomy—have affected the volume and distribution of classes ever since 1948. The capitalist class and the petty-bourgeoisie decreased, as did the Israeli proletariat. The middle classes, managers and semiautonomous classes, increased. In some but not all respects, this is reminiscent of the class structure situation in a matured capitalist country.

NOTES

1. Ben-Porat, 1986.
2. Perloff, 1963; Perloff, Dunn, Lampard, and Muthe, 1960; Wright and Singelman, 1982.
3. Wright and Singleman, 1982.
4. It is possible to estimate the absolute change in the class structure, class by class, on the basis of the general surveys in 1961, 1972, and 1983. This is of no practical importance in the present context.

8

The Class Structure in Israel:
A Summary—The Visible Hand

This study has centered on the creation and development of "class in itself" and has consciously ignored the complementary part of the old Marxian formula, that of class "for itself." Although there is mounting criticism of this apparently deterministic and linear conception of class formation, "class in itself" as indicating the creation and development of class structure is nonetheless the proper point of departure. The issue of the "in itself" perspective is unequivocal; a class is a derivative of the social structure based on and consolidated by means of positions in the society's economy. The particular content of the class structure is determined by the combination of the modes of production in a certain social formation, or society. The study of class structure formation is, as proposed in this book, the study of the structure and the derived conditions for the emergence and development of classes or more precisely, the emergence and aggregation of positions in the Israeli economy.

Accordingly, it is suggested here that structure sets limits or determines the "realm of opportunities" in a certain historical situation. This means that the particular conditions of the Israeli society at a definite period of time prescribes the class structure. Thus, not only the realm, but the nature of the limits may differ because of the particular social and historical conditions of the specific—Israeli—society. The structure as such does not select, in an anonymous manner a course of action or actions. The structure, however, allows for a range of possible outcomes, that is, a difference of position in classes. The various social agents within this structure are responsible for the selection and formation of social categories, and here for the pace and course of development of the class structure as well as for other processes of collective formation. Thus the process of class structure formation, is man made as to the means by which a class becomes a social organization and so forth.

The underlying prime process that was observed in this study was that of transition toward a capitalist system, considering the particular form that this takes in
Israeli society. The condensed history of this society heavily affected its entire
development and the particular correspondence between its economic and noneconomic instances. Class structure formation in this society was not the only process to
occur in Israel since 1948. On the contrary, the prominant process in the first and even
second decades was that of state building. The state played a crucial role in certain
critical aspects of Israeli capitalist formation and was responsible— with or
because of the particular sociohistorical conditions—for the peculiarities of the
capitalist system in Israel.

Something else is worth reemphasizing here. The process of transition toward a
capitalist system is not merely equivalent to industrialization, although it is related to and embodies it, but neither is it epitomized nor characterized solely by
this element. The process of transition towards a capitalist system may take different possible routes and forms, all with a common experience: a substantive change
in the social formation in its dominant processes of production, in its relationships of
major social categories, and its major institutions and their mutual correspondence. In
other words, changes are anticipated in the working of the economy, in the political
organizations, the legal system and so forth. This is an important theoretical and
practical point, because the changes affect the quality of social relations in the most
essential instances of a society, rather than merely causing a gradual quantitative
change. With the emerging new class structure, (as happens in transition to capitalism) the social issue is with the positions in and of production, ownership and
authority, and with benefits that these allow to some and deprive from others.
Nevertheless, the political process may predominate in a certain period, as happened in Israel, making it possible to alleviate some of the effects of immigration, of
reallocation in the class system, and of proletarization. But this is possible only
within the limits set up by the socioeconomic conditions at a conjuncture; the concrete
repertoire of the economy sets the ultimate limits. The situation in Israel was
characterized by the predominance of politics, reflecting a major degree of state
control of a large inflow of capital and over other economic and political processes.
Through certain government agencies, the hand of the state was very visible.

As delineated in this study, the class structure in Israel immediately after statehood was a prestate creation. However, the continual development of this structure
was dramatic and took place in a way that transformed the class structure and
almost every intraclass composition.

Class structure development was affected by factors that prescribed the entire
structure of the society as well as its classes. Immigration was the most critical
factor; the influx of a mass of immigrants was highly indicative of the changes that
Israeli society was undergoing. What made this an even more substantive change
was the composition of this mass immigration; immigrants with different qualities,
from different origins, and actually from different modes of production constituted
this mass immigration over the years. The effect of different departing mode(s) of

production was evident in the different proportions of highly educated immigrants, distribution of occupations, level of consolidation of the class system in the country of origin, and experience of a capitalist system. All of this was bound to affect the class structure in the country of immigration.

The outcome of this mass immigration and its composition could not be avoided. The economic base had to be modified in order to be able to absorb the increasing amount of imported labor into the limited economy of the country at that time. This was not, however, the urgent problem at the very beginning, since the critical one was that of practical absorption; providing housing and ensuring a food supply were immediate needs and then finding employment for a mainly impoverished immigrant population was necessary. In essence, a reorganization of the entire society was required, in fact, an accelerated process of state building. The class structure developing in Israel was inevitably affected by the size and composition of the immigration. For political and ideological reasons, reemigration of surplus labor or restrictions on the inflow of immigrants, such as preselection of the most qualified ones and rejection of the others was unthinkable. Hence, while the existing class structure was determined by socioeconomic conditions, the latter were heavily influenced by immigration. The point is this: The individual immigrants that were allocated to class positions constituted a major factor which through certain intermediatory processes forced changes on the class structure. As in other societies of immigration, immigrants became an implicit agent of class structure formation.

The class structure of Israeli society developed within the intertwined processes of transition toward a capitalist system and of state building. But the uniqueness of the process of transition in Israel was characterized by factors other than state building.

First, the transition's point of departure was not a feudalistic system, but already protocapitalist, encouraged during World War II, particularly in the Jewish sector in Palestine. Hence in 1948 a seminal class structure already existed. The mass immigration (and inflow of capital) almost washed out this seminal structure and erected a more complex class structure in its place. Nonetheless, this new structure was not totally different initially in its basic class composition from the prestate one, since the proletariat class and and also to certain degree the capitalist class already existed. By the late 1950s the new class structure was evident, viewing the between class composition, the increased proportion of contradictory location classes, and by the within-class composition—the ethnic, gender and religious ingredients of the classes.

Second, the agents responsible for the major processes after 1948, and in fact for the transition itself, are of critical importance. The process of transition toward capitalism was first led by the state and concomitantly by the organizations of the working class (the Histadrut, political parties) and others (Zionist organizations and other political parties). The role that was both initially and subsequently played by the state was overwhelming because of the power invested in it.

To begin with, the predominant role of the state was made possible by the peculiarity of the social structure; the political instance predominated vis-à-vis others, mainly the economy. For a very definite reason—the capital inflow to the country—the state was able to transcend the immediate limits of the economy. The state more than any other organization or institution was the major, indeed in the early 1950s the only agent of economic entrepreneurship as well as of other instances. Control of a substantive percentage of domestic capital stock and of nearly all capital inflow endowed the state with the power to become the "mover" agent in the process of transition toward capitalism.

The structural correlation of the transition to capitalism with the process of state building took the form of the practical creation of an economy through state support to the private and public sectors, by the consolidation of political and legal institutions, and so forth. A possible obstacle to the above processes, particularly to the transition toward a capitalist system, is the class structure that may constitute a barrier not only to the development and change of the economy, but also to other supporting instances. This is a problem that a state as an agent of transition has to overcome. In Israel the solution was divided into two different but related parts. First the influx of immigrants had to be reallocated in the class structure of the host society while this system was itself changing because of the influx of immigrants. The process of state building propelled the reorganization of the class structure in Israel in 1948 and forced it to readjust to the evolving modes of production; capitalist, public Histadrut, and that of the state. The mass of immigrants as the newly imported labor force made reorganization of the class structure inevitable, albeit with some measure of control by the state.

Thus the second part of the solution was state-made. It was made possible because of the following governmental advantages from 1948 on: the major power in the government, The Party of The Workers of Eretz (land) Israel (MAPAI), also enjoyed an overwhelming power in the Histadrut, the powerful organization of the working class. When other working-class parties of that time (before the creation of the labor alignment in 1965) joined the coalition headed by MAPAI, the collaboration between the government and the Histadrut increased. Thus it was possible for the government to practice a growth policy that encouraged privatization of the economy and sometimes even a wage policy that adversely affected the employees. The government was responsible more than any other factor, even the capitalist one, for the consolidation of the private sector and capitalist class in Israel. The hailed process of state building provided the ideological and political cover.

This practical conception of the state is essential for the understanding of the modern history of Israel. Within a situation of immediate pressure caused by mass immigration, meager economic capability, shortage of domestic capital, and genuine entrepreneurs, the state had to become the "factor of cohesion" as well as the agent of economic development. Indeed this was not newly unique to the regime in the 1950s. Politics as a predominant level in socioeconomic development had been experienced in the prestate period and was carried into poststatehood.

By controlling capital inflow to the country, by being able to use more capital than that taxed from the citizens, by being the major and sometimes the only, social and economic entrepreneur, the state was largely able to determine the process of class formation and the form of the working class, to mobilize this class as an agent of state building and thus to divert both potential and actual class conflict into a condition of class harmony. The state was able to encourage the development of the bourgeoisie and to enhance the latter's power in the economy. Obviously this was not totally successful. The development of the society in Israel was accompanied by internal conflicts such as those of an ethnic or religious nature, and also by a slight class conflict. Yet these were all relatively minor, although, some conflicts, like the ethnic conflict made their imprint on the society because of the overwhelming effects of the conflict between the Israeli state, the Arab states, and the stateless Palestinians.

At the end of the 1970s (even before the change in the political regime from Labor to Likud), the state started to transfer some of its possession in the economy to the private sector, thus enhancing the consolidation of a capitalist class and of a potential ground for class conflict between two pure basic classes. However, state power in the major instances of the society enabled the state to remain the major agent of the class formation process and its reproduction. It was the state, through the collusion of the political regimes in state and trade unions, that more or less neutralized the class struggle from 1948 to the 1980s.

Leaving aside for the moment the concrete effects of class and class struggle in Israel, the issue here remains the structural conditions that enabled or actually enforced the creation and development of a class structure. The term "creation" is emphasized because of the importance of this stage during the first studied period in this book. Considering the Israeli society of that time and the earlier prestate formation, it seems that this was indeed a period of some prominent transformations in society. The starting base of a population of about 650,000 was more then doubled by adding some million newcomers in about a decade. The change in the composition of the economy followed. But in line with the subject of this study the early period was singled out by the creation of a new class structure.

Its formation was evinced by the creation of positions in the economy and in other related levels of the society, that were, or were not, invested with power over investments, labor processes and labor itself. This power provided the structural matrix of the conditions of class structure. However, the process of creation of class positions was associated with another process: that of allocation of individuals to these positions. As many students of class creation who adopt the structural perspective testify, it is much easier to treat the process of *allocation* rather than that of *creation* of class positions, because evidence of the former is much more manifest than of the latter. Nonetheless, this is precisely what a structuralist perspective stands for. The development of the class structure in Israel is offered as fair support for this perspective. Judging by appearances, ethnicity, gender and other ingredients of social formations constitute causes of division of labor in this society. This is indeed so, but the prime cause of the division of labor in Israel was based on the emerging class structure. Even if it was not explicit in the political agenda, this structure was and continued to be the prime factor preceding or accompanying any other factor of social distribution.

The data on the formation of class structure in Israel are instructive. During the four decades, the capitalist class changed very little. The petty-bourgeois class decreased, as did the proletariat, which lost its relative majority. The "new middle class" as some writers like to name the growing share of managers, experts and technicians, became proportionately the predominant class. This seems to be a direct outcome of the economic growth and change that took place.

The class-cum-other competitive bases of formation also changed. Gender, ethnic origin and religion/nationality had, and still have, a discriminatory effect on allocation to class positions. In social terms minority categories behaved in Israel like minorities in other capitalist or quasi-capitalist countries. Being a female, a Sephardi, or an Arab, *cetaris paribus*, made one less likely, and sometimes very unlikely, to gain a capitalist position or become a manager or professional Entering the proletariat is more likely if the above ingredients dominate. Being an Arab in Israel, even as a citizen, is far less advantageous than being a Jew. As in other capitalist societies the process of allocation to class position is influenced by merit factors such as education. However, even these factors could not eliminate the effects of gender, ethnicity, and religion. Probably the accelerated growth of the Israeli economy and certain technological changes overcame these factors to some extent and weakened their influence on class positions allocation. Thus those structural conditions that formulate the entire Israeli society also set limits on class structure formation and its correlation with other bases of social formation.

The partition of the overall period into three subperiods was prescribed because of the nature and availability of the data. However, the sociohistorical rationale of this partition is substantive; these subperiods indicate basic stages in the structural conditions that molded the development of a class structure in Israel. Thus the first subperiod is characterized by a surge in the size of certain classes, by the highly effective influence of the state on class structure formation, and by a deep change in the composition of the classes after 1948. The second period is characterized by the start of stabilization of the class structure under the still accelerating conditions of socioeconomic growth. This was interrupted by some of the consequences of the Six Days War, with the entrance of Arab labor from the occupied territories, and with the export of Israeli goods and capital to these territories. The class structure of the 1980s was appropriately affected by this situation as is observed in the size of the proletariat.

The entire class structure formation since 1948 could be portrayed as a process of emergence from a temporary and vague situation into some sort of stabilization through growth in the socioeconomic structure and the subjection of the reserve labor of Arabs in the territories. Before concluding this issue there are some other points that must be reassessed here.

It has been previously claimed that the class structure in Israel in the 1980s is similar to that of a capitalist society, and in practice, to that of the United States. This is so regarding the specific classes in the class structure and the estimated distribution of positions in the fivefold class scheme. However, when this is scrutinized more closely, the following reservations seem necessary. All are derived from the fact that the sociohistorical specificity of Israel made some difference. First, the class structure of Israel is heavily determined by the coexistence of different modes of production; state, public Histadrut, and capitalist. This must have some effects on the class structure, for example, on the positions of capitalists. The formal statistics used here do not disclose the positions that can be termed "state capitalist" or "Histadrut capitalist." However inappropriate these terms seem, they indicate the lack of more refined information on class positions. This was taken into consideration in other studies such as the study which compares the Swedish class structure to that of the United States Unfortunately, this approach was precluded in this study. Second, while looking into the composition of the class structure in Israel, one observes some differences between Israel and the United States, such as the composition by gender, or even by ethnic factor. It appears that class-cum-gender composition in Israel is quite different from that of the United States The percentage of women capitalists in Israel is much less than in the United States. Also, women in Israel do not predominate in the working class. Hence the process of allocation into class positions is different from that in the United States Nonetheless, given the above qualifications, the claim of similarity between the class structure in Israel and capitalist societies is valid.

Another point of comparison is the share of contradictory locations in both societies. Taking into account the differences in measuring classes, it appears that the percentages of contradictory locations in Israel are still higher than in the United States. Probably this can be partly explained by the different stages of capitalism in the two societies; the United States is a matured capitalist system, while Israel is still in a transitional stage, and its social formation contains different modes of production. All in all, the class structure of Israeli society in the 1980s is very close to that of a capitalist system, in theory—as the model of class structure suggests, and in practice—as the evidence on class positions indicates.

This study started with a presentation of the major socioeconomic parameters of the Israeli society, that are assumed to constitute the content of the "realm of opportunities." It proposed that these are the limits of the conditions for the emergence and development of the structure. The gist of this study centered on the presentation of the class structure in the three subperiods and the process of allocation to class positions, and, to some extent, the creation of class structure positions. It was proposed that the development of the class structure by the range of classes in a conjuncture, as well as by the composition of each existing class, is determined by the above-stated limits. Thus it is argued here that structural changes are responsible for the stability of, or change in, the class structure. In the conventional usage of sociology, this is what has to be established. Following the general thrust of causal relations, it was necessary to discuss correlation and causation in order to draw conclusions on the relations between socioeconomic conditions and the class structure since 1948. In order to establish the causal relations this study used the concept of structural causation and periodical analysis of socioeconomic conditions with the structure of the classes at the certain subperiod. It does appear that the major parameters of the society's structure were responsible for the development of the class structure. Other parameters neither mentioned nor taken into account (because of the selection of major issues, or because of the methodology that was optioned) may also share some responsibility, and so one has to admit that this study could not cover every single factor even though it covers most of the important ones.

Israel in the 1980s is in a state of multifaceted tension. There are conflicts between Jews and Arabs, the religious and the secular, the Left and the Right. It appears, therefore, that the the practical notion of class is outmoded. Class struggle does not really exist at the present time in the Israeli society. The formation of class as "class for itself" is not at the top of the political agenda. Other issues dominate the politics of the country. Yet ever since statehood the class structure as "class in itself" has constituted a prime process. A society that underwent and still is undergoing, a process of transition toward a capitalist system, cannot avoid the most prime effect of this process—the formation of a new division of labor through the organization and reorganization of the class structure.

References

(H) indicates a publication in the Hebrew language.

Achdut Lea, Y. Tamir, and Yehuda Geva. 1979. "Changes in the Patterns of Poverty in Israel 1968-1975." Jerusalem: the Institute for National Security Research, No. 22.

Adler, Israel, and Robert W. Hodge. 1983. "Ethnicity and the Process of Status Attainment." *Israel Social Science Research*, 1:5-23.

Aharoni, Yair. 1976. *Structure and Performance in The Israeli Economy*. Tel Aviv: Gome. (H)

Aharoni, Yair. 1979. *State-Owned Enterprises in Israel and Abroad*. Tel Aviv: Gome. (H)

Aldrich H. John, and Nelson D. Forrest. 1984. *Linear Probability, Logit and Probit Models*. Beverly Hills: Sage.

Althusser, Louis, and Etienne Balibar. 1970. *Reading Capital*. London: New Left Books.

Aminzade, Ronald. 1984. "Re-Interpreting Capitalist Industrialization; A Study of Nineteenth Century France." *Social History*, 9:329-50.

Aminzade, Ronald, and Randy Hodson. 1982. "Social Mobility in a Mid-Nineteenth Century French City." *American Sociological Review*, 47:441-57.

Amir, Shmuel. 1986. "Educational Structure and Wage Differentials of the Labor Force in the 1970s" in: Ben-Porath Y, (ed), *The Israeli Economy: Maturing Through Crises*. Cambridge, Mass.: Harvard University Press, 137-52.

Anderson, Perry. 1980. *Arguments Within Marxism*. London: New Left Books.

Arnon, Arieh. 1986-70 "Israel-US Relations, 1967-1985: The Economic Aspects and Beyond." Beersheva: Discussion paper No. 14, Department of Economics and The Monaster Center for Economic Research, Ben-Gurion University of the Negev.

Avnimelech, Moriya. 1974. "The Influence of Public Expenditure on Social Services on the Redistribution of Incomes." *Social Security* Jerusalem, 6-7, 72-86.

Bahral, Uri. 1965. "The Effect of Mass Immigration on Wages In Israel." Jerusalem: The Maurice Falk Institute for Economic Research in Israel.

Bank of Israel. *Annual Report.* Jerusalem: Various Years.

Barkai, Haim. 1977. "Growth Pattern of The Kibbutz Industry." Contribution to Economic Analysis. North-Holland.

Barkai, Haim. 1983. "The Genesis of the Israeli Economy." Jerusalem: The Maurice Falk Institute for Economic Research in Israel. (H)

Barkai, Haim. 1984. "The Public, Histadrut and Private Sectors in the Israeli Economy." Jerusalem: The Maurice Falk Institute for Economic Research in Israel, Sixth Report.

Barkai, Haim. 1986. "Thought on Present Day Economic Growth In Israel". Israel: *Banking Quarterly*, 95:74-92. (H)

Barkai, Haim. 1987. "Israel's Attempt At Economic Stabilization." Jerusalem: Falk Institute for Economic Research in Israel, Research Paper No. 195.

Barkai, Haim. 1987b. "Kibbutz Efficiency and the Incentive Conundrum." Jerusalem: The Maurice Falk Institute for Economic Research in Israel, Research Paper, No. 196.

Beck, E. M., Patrick M. Horan, and Charles. M. Tolbert II. 1978. "Stratification in a Dual Economy; A Sectoral Model of Earnings Determination." *American Sociological Review*, 43:704-20.

Becker, E. H. 1984. "Self-Employed Worker; An Update to 1983." *Monthly Labor Review*, (July):14-18.

Ben-Porat, Amir. 1979. "Union Democracy; Political Parties and Democracy in The Histadrut." *Industrial Relations*, 18:237-43.

Ben-Porat, Amir. 1986. *Between Class and Nation.* Connecticut: Greenwood Press.

Ben-Porat, Amir. 1986/87. "The Formation of the Working Class; A Comparative Study of the Formation of the Working Class in America and Palestine 1881-1920." *Science and Society*, 4: 26-43.

Ben-Porat, Amir. 1987. "Becoming Proletariate; Immigrants In Israel 1948-1961." Beersheva: Dept. of Behavioural Sciences, Ben-Gurion University of the Negev.

Ben-Porat, Amir. 1987b. "Class Consciousness Before Class." *Theory and Society*, 16:741-69.

Ben-Porat, Amir. 1989. "Political Domination and Reproduction of Classless Organization." *Economic and Industrial Democracy*, 10:151-164.

Ben-Porath, Yoram. 1966. "The Arab Labor Force in Israel." Jerusalem: The Maurice Falk Institute for Economic Research in Israel.

Ben-Porath, Yoram. 1986. "Self-Employed and Wage Earners in Israel; Findings from the Census of Population, 1972." in O. Uziel Shmeltz, and Gad Nathan eds. *Studies in the Population of Israel*. Jerusalem: Magnes Press, 245-80.

Ben-Porath, Yoram, ed. 1986 *The Israeli Economy; Maturing Through Crises.* Cambridge, Mass.: Harvard University Press.

Ben-Porath, Yoram. 1986. "The Entwined Growth of Population and Product 1922-1982." In Y. Ben-Porath, ed., 27-41.

Ben-Porath, Yoram. 1986. "Diversity in Population and in The Labor Force." In Y. Ben-Porath, ed.,153-70.

Bernstein, Deborah. 1981. "Immigrant Transit Camps - The Formation of Dependent Relations in Israeli Society." *Ethnic and Racial Studies*, 4:440-63.

Bernstein, Deborah. 1987. *The Struggle For Equality; Women Workers in the Palestine "Yishuv"*. Tel Aviv: Hakibbutz Hameuchad.

Bernstein, Deborah, and Shlomo Swirski. 1982. "The Rapid Economic Development of Israel and the Emergence of Ethnic Division of Labour." *British Journal of Sociology*, 33:64-85.

Bodnar, John. 1977. *Immigration and Industrialization; Ethnicity in An American Mill Town 1870-1940*. Pittsburg: University of Pittsburg Press.

Bonacich, Edna. 1976. "Advanced Capitalism and Black/White Relations in the United States; A Split Labor Market Interpretation." *American Sociological Review*, 34-51.

Bonne, Alfred. 1948. *State and Economics in the Middle East; A Society in Transition*. London: Kegan Paul.

Bonne, Alfred. 1959. "Trends in Occupational Structure and Distribution of Income Among The Jewish Piopulation in Israel." *Jewish Journal of Sociology*, 1:242-49.

Braverman, Harry. 1974. *Labor and Monopoly Capitalism*. New York: Monthly Review Press.

Brenner, Robert. 1976. "Agrarian Class Structure and Economic Development in Pre-Industrial Europe." *Past and Present*, 70:30-75.

Britten, N., and A. Heat. 1983. "Women, Men and Social Class." In E. Gamarnikow et al., eds. *Gender, Class and Work*. London: Heinemann.

Bronschier, Volker, Christopher Chase-Donne, and Richard Robinson. "Cross National Evidence of the Effect of Foreign Investment and on Economic Growth and Inequality: A Survey of Findings and Analysis." *American Journal of Sociology*, 84:651-83.

Burawoy, Michael. 1985. *The Politics of Production*. London: New Left Books.

Carchedi, Guglielmo. 1977. *On the Economic Identification of Social Classes*. London: Routledge and Kegan Paul.

Carmi, Shulamit and Henry Rosenfeld. 1974. "The Origins of the Process of Proletarization and Urbanization of Arab Peasants in Palestine."Annals of New York Academy of Sciences.

Carter, Bob. 1986. Review of E. O. Wright. "Classes." *Sociological Review*, 34:686-88.

Castels, Stephen and Godula Kosack. 1973. *Immigrant Workers and Class Structure in Western Europe*. London: Oxford University Press.

Central Bureau of Statistics (CBS). *Statistical Abstracts of Israel, 1960-1986*. Jerusalem: various dates.

Central Bureau of Statistics (CBS). *Labor Force Surveys*. Jerusalem: various years.

Central Bureau of Statistics (CBS). *Special Publications Series.* Jerusalem: various years.

Chenery, Holis, and Moshe Syrquin. 1975. *Pattern of Development 1950-1970.* London: Oxford University Press.

Chenery, Holis, Sherman Robinson, and Moshe Syrquin. 1986. *Industrialization and Growth; A Comparative Study.* London: Oxford University Press.

Chilcote H. Ronald, and Dale L. Johnson, eds. 1983. *Theories of Development.* Beverly-Hills, Calif.: Sage.

Cohen, G, A. 1978. *Karl Marx Theory of History: A Defence.* Princeton, New Jersey: Princeton University Press.

Crompton, Rosemary, and Michael Mann, eds. 1986. *Gender and Stratification.* Cambridge: Polity Press.

Cuneo, C. J. 1984. "Has the Traditional Petite Bourgeoisie Persisted?" *The Canadian Journal of Sociology,* 9:269-301.

Dale, A. 1986. "Social Class and the Self Employed." *Sociology,* 20:430-34.

Daniel, Abraham. 1976. *Labor Enterprises in Israel.* Jerusalem: Academic Press.

Duke, Vic, and Stephen Edgell. 1987."The Operationalisation of Class in British Sociology; Theoretical and Empirical Considerations." *The British Journal of Sociology,* 38:445-63.

Duncan, Otis Dudley. 1966. "Occupational Trends and Patterns of Net Mobility." *Demography,* 3:1-18.

Duncan, Otis Dudley. 1966. "Methodological Issues in the Analysis of Social Mobility." In J. Neil Smelser, and Seymor M. Lipset. *Social Structure and Mobility in Economic Development.* Chicago, Ill.: Aladine, 51-97.

Ehrenreich, Barbara and John Ehrenreich. 1971. "The Professional-Managerial Class." *Radical America,* 1.

Eisenstadt, N. Shmuel. 1966. *Modernization, Protest and Change.* Englewood Cliffs, N.J.: Prentice Hall, 1966.

Eisenstadt, N. Shmuel. 1985. *The Transformation of Israeli Society.* London: Weidenfeld and Nicolson.

Erikson, Robert. 1984. "Social Class of Men and Families." *Sociology,* 18:500-514.

Erikson, Robert, John H. Goldthorpe, and Lucienne Portocarero. 1982. "Social Fluidity in Industrial Nations; England, France and Sweden." *British Journal of Sociology,* 33:1-34.

Etzioni, Amitai. 1983. *An Immodest Agenda; Rebuilding America Before the Twenty First Century.* New York: McGraw-Hill.

Evans, M. D. R., and J. Kelley. 1984. "Immigrants' Work; Equality and Discrimination in the Australian Labour Market." Canberra: The Australian and New Zealand Association for Advancement of Science.

Even-Shoshan Orit, 1985. Yoram Gabbay, and Yaacov Kop. "Family Incidence of Income and Taxes." *The Economic Quarterly,* 35(127):334-353.

Foley, K. Duncan. 1978. "State Expenditure from a Marxist Perspective." *Journal of Public Economics,* 9:221-38.

Foster-Carter, Aidan. 1978. "The Mode of Production Controversy." *New Left Review,* 107:47-78.

Gaathon, A. L. 1971. *Economic Productivity in Israel.* New York, Washington, and London: Praeger.

Giddens, Anthony. 1973. *The Class Structure of the Advanced Societies.* London: Hutchinson.

Giddens, Anthony. 1985. Review of E. O. Wright, "Classes" in *New Society,* 29:383-84.

Ginor, Fanny. 1979. *Socio-Economic Disparities In Israel.* Tel-Aviv: Horovitz Institution.

Goldthorpe, John. 1980. *Social Mobility and Class Structure in Modern Britain.* Oxford: Clarendon Press.

Goldthorpe, John. 1982. "On the Service Class; Its Formation and Future" in Anthony Giddens, and G. Mackenzie, eds. *Social Class and the Division of Labour.* Cambridge: Cambridge University Press.

Goldthorpe, John. 1983. "Women and Class Analysis; In Defence of the Conventional View." *Sociology,* 7:465-88.

Goran, Ahrne. 1981. "The Swedish Class Structure; Comparative Project on Class structure and Class Consciousness." Madison: University of Wisconsin, Dept. of Sociology, Working Paper No. 4.

Goran, Ahrne, and Erik Olin Wright. 1983. "Classes in the United States and Sweden; A Comparison." *Acta Sociologica,* 26.

Gorin, Zeev. 1984. "Income Inequality in Marxist Theory of Development." In F. R. Tomasson, ed. *Comparative Social Research.* Greenwich: JAI Press, 147-74.

Habermas, Jurgan. 1975. *Legitimation Crisis.* Boston: Beacon Press.

Haberman, J. Shelby. 1978/79. *Analysis of Qualitative Data.* New York: Academic Press, Nos. 1 and 2.

Haberman. J. Shelby. 1982. "Analysis of Dispersion of Multinomial Responses." *Journal of the American Statistical Association,* 77:568-80.

Halevi, Nadav. 1986. "Perspectives on the Balance of Payments." In, Y. Ben-Porath, ed. 242-63.

Halevi, Nadav, and Ruth Klinov-Malul. 1968. *The Economic Development of Israel.* New York: Praeger.

Hanoch, Giora. 1961. "Income Differentials in Israel." Jerusalem: The Maurice Falk Institute for Economic Research in Israel, Fifth Report, 1959-1960.

Handlin, Oscar. 1973. *The Uprooted.* Boston: Little Brown and Company.

Hartman, Moshe. 1981. "International Migration, Social Status and Ethnic Stratification." Paris: ISA Research Seminar on Stratification, 1981..

Hartmann, Heidi. 1976. "Capitalism, Patriarchy and Job Segregation By Sex." In Martin Blaxall, and Barbara Reagan, eds. *Woman and Workplace.* Chicago: University of Chicago Press.

Hartmann, Heidi. 1981. "The Unhappy Marriage of Marxism and Feminism; Toward a More Progressive Union." In L. Sargent, ed. *Women and Revolution.* London: Plateau Press.

Hauser, M. Robert, Peter J. Dickinson, Harry P. Travis and John H. Koffel. 1975. "Structural Changes in Occupational Mobility Among Men in the United States." *American Sociological Review,* 40:585-98.

Hauser, M. Robert, and L. David Featherman. 1977.*The Process of Stratification; Trends and Analysis.* New York: Academic Press.

Hazelring, Lawrence E., and Maurice A. Garnier. 1976. "Occupational Mobility in Industrial Societies; A Comparative Analysis of Differential Access to Occupational Ranks in Seventeen Countries." *American Sociological Review,* 41:498-511.

Heat, A., and N. Britten. 1984. "Women's Jobs Do Make A Difference; A Reply to Goldthorpe." *Sociology,* 18.

Hercowitz, Z. 1976. "The Stock of Education Capital in Israel and its Distribution, 1961-1971." Jerusalem: The Maurice Falk Institute for Economic Research In Israel, Discussion Paper, No. 76.09. (H)

Hindess, Barry, and Paul Hirst. 1977. *Modes of Production and Social Formation.* London: Routledge and Kegan Paul.

Hirst, Fred, and John H. Goldthorpe. 1978. *The Political Economy of Inflation.* Cambridge, Mass.: Harvard University Press.

Hobsbawm, Eric. 1968. *Pre-Capitalist Economic Formation.* New York: International Publishers,.

Hobsbawm, Eric. 1969. *Industry and Empire.* Baltimore: Penguin Books.

Hodge, W. Robert. 1973. "Toward a Theory of Racial Differences in Employment." *Social Forces,* 52:16-31.

Horowitz Dan, and Moshe Lissak. 1977.*The Origins of The Israeli State.* Tel Aviv: Am-Oved.

Horowitz, David. 1972. *The Enigma of Economic Growth; A Case Study of Israel.* New York: Praeger.

Howe, Irving. 1976. *The World of Our Fathers.* New York: Harcourt, Brace, Jovanovich.

Institute for Economic and Social Research.1964. *Strikes and Lockouts, 1950-1964.* Tel Aviv: Histadrut.

Institute For Economic and Social Research. 1985. *Strikes in Israel, 1974-1984.* Tel Aviv: Histadrut.

Jackman, Robert. 1975. *Politics and Equality.* New York: Wiley.

Johnson, L. Dale, ed. 1985. *Middle Classes in Dependent Countries.* Beverly Hills, Calif.: Sage.

Kalenberg, L Arne, and Aage B. Sorensen. 1979. "The Sociology of Labour Markets." *Annual Review of Sociology,* 5:351-79.

Kerr, Clark, John T. Dunlop, Frederick H. Harbison and Charles A. Myers. 1960. *Industrialism and Industrial Man.* Cambridge, Mass.: Harvard University Press.

Kleinman, Ephraim. "The Histadrut Economy of Israel; In Search of Criteria." The Jerusalem Quarterly, 1987, 41: 77-94.

Klinov-Malul, Ruth. 1976. "Changes in Occupational Structure of the Labor Force, 1960-1974." in N. Halevi, and Y. Kop, eds. "Issues in the Economy of Israel." Jerusalem: The Maurice Falk Institute for Economic Development in Israel.

Klinov-Malul, Ruth. 1986. "Changes in The Industrial Structure." In Y. Ben-Porath, ed. The Israeli Economy. Cambridge, Mass.: Harvard University Press, 119-36.

Klinov-Malul, Ruth. 1986. "The Work Force in Israel, 1948-1984." Jerusalem: The Maurice Falk Institute for Economic Development in Israel. Discussion Paper No. 84.04. (H)

Knoke, David and Peter J. Burk. 1980. Log-linear Models. Beverly Hills, Calif.: Sage.

Kolko, Gabriel. 1967. Wealth and Power in America. New York: Praeger.

Kop, Jacob. 1985. Allocation of Resources to Social Services. Jerusalem: The Center for the study of Social Policy in Israel.

Kraus, Vered. 1982. "Ethnic Origin as Hierarchical Dimension of Social Status and Its Correlates." Sociology and Social Research, 66:252-66.

Kuznetz, Simon. 1955. "Economic Growth and Income Inequality." American Economic Review, 45:1-28.

Kuznetz, Simon. 1965. Economic Growth and Structure; Selected Essays. New York: W. W. North.

Kuznetz, Simon. 1966. Modern Economic Growth; Rate, Structure and Spread. New Haven: Yale University Press, 1966.

Lamdany, Reuben. 1982. "Emigration from Israel." Jerusalem: The Maurice Falk Institute for Economic Development in Israel, Discussion Paper, 82.08.

Leachman, Robert. 1976. The Age of Keynes. New York: Random House.

Lewin-Epstein, Noah, and Moshe Semyonov. 1986. "Ethnic Group Mobility in the Israeli Labor Market." American Sociological Review, 51:342-51.

Liberson, Stanley. 1970. "Stratification and Ethnic Groups." Sociological Inquiry, 40:172-81.

Lipset, S. Martin, and Hans Zetterberg. 1959. "Social Mobility in Industrial Societies." In S. Martin Lipset, and Reinhard Bendix. 1959. Social Mobility in Industrial Society. London: Heinemann.

Lissak, Moshe, Beverly Mizrachi, and Ofra Ben David. 1969.Immigrants in Israel. Jerusalem: Academon.

Marx, Karl. 1971. The Poverty of Philosophy. New York: International Publications.

Matras, Judah. 1963/64. "Some Data on Intergenerational Occupational Mobility in Israel." Public Studies 17:167-86.

Matras, Judah. 1965. Social Change in Israel. Chicago, Ill.: Aladine.

Matras, Judah, G. Noam, and Y. Bar-Haim. 1984. "Israeli Educated Men in the Transition To Adulthood; Patterns of Schooling, Military Service and Employment." Jerusalem: Mimeograph.

Mayhew, M. Bruce. 1981. "Structuralism Versus Individualism." Part 1, "Shadow-boxing in the Dark." *Social Forces*, 59(2):335-75.

Mayhew, M. Bruce. 1981. "Structuralism Versus Individualism." Part 2, "Ideological and Other Obfuscations." *Social Forces*, 59(3):627-48.

Mayshar, Yoram. 1986. "Investment Patterns." In Y. Ben-Porath, ed., 101-18.

Merriman, M. John, ed. 1979. *Consciousness and Class Experience in Nineteenth Century Europe.* New York: Holms-Meier Publishers.

Metzer, Jacob. 1986. "The Slowdown of Economic Growth; A Passing Phase or the End or the Big Spurt?" In Y. Ben-Porath, ed. *The Israeli Economy: Maturing Through Crises.* Cambridge, Mass.: Harvard University Press, 73-100.

Miller, C. Delbert, and William H. Form. 1980. *Industrial Sociology.* New York: Harper and Row.

Nahon, Jacob. 1987. "Trends in Employment - The Ethnic Dimension." Jerusalem: The Jerusalem Institute for the Study of Israel.

Neuman, Shoshana, and Adrian Ziderman. 1986. "Testing the Dual Labor Market Hypothesis; Evidence from the Israel Labor Mobility Survey." *The Journal of Human Resources*, 230-37.

O'Connor, James. 1973. *The Fiscal Crisis of The State.* New York: St. Martin Press.

Ofer, Gur. 1967. *The Service Industries in a Developing Economy; Israel as a Case Study.* New York: Praeger.

Ofer, Gur, and Y. Ben-Porath ed. 1986. "Public Spending On Civilian Services." 192-208.

Offe, Claus, and Von Beyem, ed. 1974. "Structural Problems of the Capitalist State." In *German Political Studies*, Vol. 1, Beverly Hills, Calif.: Sage, 31-57.

Pack, Howard. 1971. *Structural Change and Economic Policy in Israel.* New Haven, Conn.: Yale University Press.

Patenkin, Dan. 1967. "The Israeli Economy; The First Decade." Jerusalem: The Maurice Falk Institute for Economic Research in Israel.

Peres, Yochanan. 1971. "Ethnic Relations in Israel." *American Journal of Sociology*, 76:1021-47.

Perloff, S. Harvey. 1963. "How A Region Grows." Supplementary Paper No. 17, Committee For Economic Development, March.

Perloff, S. Harvey, E. S. Dunn, E. E. Lampard and R. F. Muthe. 1960. *Regions, Resources, and Economic Growth.* Baltimore: Johns Hopkins Press.

Peterson, Trond. 1985. "A Comment on Presenting Results From Logit and Probit Models." *American Sociological Review*, 50:130-31.

Piory, J. Michael. 1975. "Notes For the Theory of Labor Market Stratification." In C Richard Edwards, Michael Reich, and David M. Gordon, eds. *Labor Market Segmentation.* Lexington: Heat, 125-50.

Piory, J. Michael. 1979. *Birds of Passage.* Cambridge Mass.: Cambridge University Press.

Piory, J. Michael, and Charles F. Sobel. 1984. *The Second Industrial Divide.* New Jersey: Basic Books.

Portes, Alejandro, and Alex Stepnick. 1985. "Unwelcome Immigrants; The Labor Market Experience of 1980. Cuban and Haitian Refugees in South Florida." *American Sociological Review*, 50:493-514.

Poulantzas, Nicos. 1973. *Political Power and Social Classes*. London: New Left Books.

Poulantzas, Nicos. 1975. *Classes in Contemporary Capitalism*. London: New Left Books.

Prezeworski, Adam. 1977. "The Process of Class Formation from Karl Kautsky's 'The Class Struggle' to Recent Debates." *Politics and Society*, 7:343-401.

Prezeworski, Adam. 1985. *Capitalism and Social Democracy*. Cambridge: Cambridge University Press.

Razin, Assaf. 1983. "U.S. Foreign Aid To Israel." *The Jerusalem Quarterly*, 29:11-19.

Reynolds, Morgan, and Eugene Smolensky. 1977. *Public Expenditures, Taxes and The Distribution of Income; The U. S., 1950, 1961, 1971*. New York: Academic Press.

Robinson, V. Robert. 1984. "Structural Change and Class Mobility in Capitalist Societies." *Social Forces*, 63:51-71.

Rose, David, and Marshall Gordon. 1986. "Constructing the (W)right Classes." *Sociology*, 20:440-45.

Rosenblum, Gerald. 1973. *Immigrant Workers; Their Impact on American Labor Radicalism*. New Jersey: Basic Books.

Rosenfeld, Henry. 1962. "The Arab Village Proletariate." *New Outlook*, 5:7-17.

Rosenfeld, Henry. 1977. *The Class Position of the Arab Minority in Israel*. Haifa: Machbarot L'Bikoret Haifa, University of Haifa.

Rustum, Bastumi. 1973. "The Arab in Israel." In Michael Curtis, and Mordechai Chertoff, eds. *Israel; Social Structure and Change*. New Brunswick, N.J.: Transaction Books.

Scott, John, 1979. *Corporations, Classes and Capitalism*. New York: St. Martin's Press.

Segev, Tom. 1984. *1949—The Israelis*. Jerusalem: Domino Press.

Sewitzer, Avram. 1984. *Upheavals*. Jerusalem: Bitan Zmora and Jerusalem Institute for Israel Studies, Tel Aviv.

Sharkansky, Ira. 1979. *Whither the State?* New Jersey: Chatham House.

Shelhev, Joseph, and Menachem Freidman. 1985. "Growth and Segregation, The Ultra Orthodox Community in Jerusalem." Jerusalem: The Jerusalem Institute for Israel Studies.

Shetzer, Yael. 1987. "Foreign Capital in Israel." seminar paper. Beersheba: Department of Behavioral Sciences, Ben-Gurion University.

Sicron, Moshe. 1957. "Immigration to Israel 1948-1953." Jerusalem: Israel Central Bureau of Statistics, No. 60.

Simkus, Albert. 1984. "Structural Transformation and Social Mobility; Hungary 1938-1973." *American Sociological Review*, 49:291-307.

Simpson, Ida Harper, Richard L. Simpson, Mark Evers and Sharon Sandomirsky. 1982. "Occupational Recruitment, Retention, and Labor Force Cohort Representation." *American Journal of Sociology*, 87:1287-313.

Singelman, Joachim. 1978. *From Agriculture to Service*. Beverly Hills, Calif.: Sage.

Singelman, Joachim. 1987. "Class structure and the Organization of Service Industries in West Germany 1985". Paper presented at the GOP meeting, Antwerp, Belgium.

SPSSX. 1986. *User's Guide.* New York: McGraw-Hill.

Smoocha, Sammy. 1978. *Israel; Pluralism and Conflict.* Berkeley: University of California Press.

Stephens, D. John. 1979. *The Transition From Capitalism To Socialism.* London: Macmillan.

Stewart, A., K. Prandy, and R. M. Blackburn.1980. *Social Stratification and Occupations.* New York: Holms and Meier.

Strinati, Dominic. 1979."Capitalism, The State and Industrial Relations." in Colin Crouch, ed. *State and Economy in Contemporary Capitalism.* New York: St. Martin's Press, 191-236.

Sweezy, Paul. 1942. *The Theory of Capitalist Development.* New York: Monthly Review Press.

Syrquin, Moshe. 1986 "Economic Growth and Structural Change; An International Perspective." In Y. Ben-Porath, ed., 42-74.

Syrquin, Moshe. 1984. "Economic Growth and Structural Change; Israel in an International Perspective." Jerusalem: Maurice Falk Institute for Economic Development in Israel. Discussion Paper No. 84.08.

Taylor, C. Lewis, and C. Michael Hudson. 1972. *World Handbook of Political and Social Indicators.* New Haven and London: Yale University Press.

Taylor, G. John. 1979. *From Modernization to Modes of Production; A Critique of the Sociologies of Development and Underdevelopment.* New Jersey: Humanities Press.

Thompson, E. P. 1963. *The Making of the English Working Class.* New York: Pantheon Books.

Thompson, E. P. 1978. *The Poverty of Theory and Other Essays.* London: Monthly Review Press.

Toivonen, Timo.1987. "The Rise of Self-Employment and Industrial Structure." Antwerp: EGOS Colloquium.

Tilly, Charles, ed. 1975. *The Formation of National States In Western Europe.* Princeton, N. J.: Princeton University Press.

Tilly, Charles. 1983. "Flow of Capital and Forms of Industry in Europe, 1500-1900." *Theory and Society,* 12:123-42.

Turner, B. 1975. *Industrialism.* Harlow: Longman.

Tyree, Andrea. 1973. "Mobility Ratios and Association in Mobility Tables." *Population Studies,* 577-88.

Tyree, Andrea. 1981. "Occupational Socio-Economic Status. Ethnicity and Sex in Israel; Consideration in Scale Construction." *Megamot,* 27:7-21. (H)

West, J., ed. *Women, Work and the Labour Market.* London: Routledge and Kegan Paul.

Wright, E. Olin. 1978. *Class, Crisis and the State.* London: New Left Books.

Wright, E. Olin. 1980. "Varieties of Marxist Conceptions of Class Structure." *Politics and Society,* 9:3:323-70.

Wright, E. Olin. 1983. "Capitalism's Future; A Provisional Reconceptualization of Alternatives to Capitalist Society." *Socialist Review,* 68:77-126.

Wright, E. Olin. 1983. "What is Neo and What is Marxist in Neo-Marxist Class Analysis?" Working paper, Comparative Project on Class Structure and Class Consciousness. Madison: University of Wisconsin, Dept. of Sociology.

Wright, E. Olin. 1985. *Classes.* London: New Left Books.

Wright, E. Olin. 1985."The Fall and Rise of the Petty Bourgeoisie; Class Structure and Class Consciousness." Project Working paper, Madison: University of Wisconsin, Dept. of Sociology.

Wright, E. Olin, Cynthia Costello, David Hachen, and Joy Sprague. 1982. "The American Class Structure." *American Sociological Review,* 47:709-26.

Wright, E. Olin, and Joachim Singelmann. 1982. "Proletarization in Changing American Class Structure." In Michael Burawoy and Teda Skocpol, eds. *Marxist Inquiries; Studies of Labor, Class and States.* Chicago, Ill.: The University of Chicago Press, 176-209.

Wilensky, Harold. 1975. *The Welfare State and Equality.* Berkeley and Los Angeles: University of California Press

Wilensky, Harold. 1976. *The "New Corporatism", Centralization and the Welfare State.* Beverly Hills, Calif.: Sage.

Williamson, Jeffrey, and Peter Lindret. 1980. *American Inequality.* New York: Academic Press.

Wolpe, Harold, ed. 1980. *The Articulation of Modes of Production.* London: Routledge and Kegan Paul.

Yariv, D. 1984. "Estimation of the Public's Wealth and Its Development from 1970 to 1982." Jerusalem: Bank of Israel Research Department, Discussion paper No. 84.10.

Yitzhaki, Shlomo. 1986. "On Stratification and Inequality by Continent of Origin In Israel." Jerusalem: The Maurice Falk Institute for Economic Development in Israel, Discussion Paper, No. 86.05.

Zuriek, Elia T. 1976. "Transformation of Class Structure Among the Arabs in Israel; From Peasantry to Proletariate." *Journal of Palestine Studies,* 6(1).

Index

About the Author

AMIR BEN-PORAT is Senior Lecturer in the Department of Behavior Sciences, Ben-Gurion University of the Negev, Israel. He received his education in Israel and the United Kingdom, and is the author of *Between Class and Nation* (Greenwood Press, 1986). Ben-Porat's articles have appeared in *International Journal of Comparative Sociology* and *Science and Society*.